Game Design and Intelligent Interaction

Edited by Ioannis Deliyannis

Published in London, United Kingdom

IntechOpen

Supporting open minds since 2005

Game Design and Intelligent Interaction
http://dx.doi.org/10.5772/intechopen.77403
Edited by Ioannis Deliyannis

Contributors
Maksims Kornevs, Jannicke Baalsrud Hauge, Sebastiaan Meijer, Katherine Smith, Yuzhong Shen, Anthony Dean, Mirko Suznjevic, Maja Homen, Mifrah Ahmad, Zuzana Václavíková, Francesco De Pace, Andrea Sanna, Federico Manuri, Iñigo Lerga Valencia, Dionysios Manesis, Adrián Domínguez, Daniel Vallés, Luis de Marcos, Juan Aguado, Sergio Caro

First published in London, United Kingdom, 2020 by IntechOpen
IntechOpen is the global imprint of INTECHOPEN LIMITED, registered in England and Wales, registration number: 11086078, 7th floor, 10 Lower Thames Street, London, EC3R 6AF, United Kingdom
Printed in Croatia

British Library Cataloguing-in-Publication Data
A catalogue record for this book is available from the British Library

Additional hard and PDF copies can be obtained from orders@intechopen.com

Game Design and Intelligent Interaction
Edited by Ioannis Deliyannis
p. cm.
Print ISBN 978-1-83880-009-3
Online ISBN 978-1-83880-010-9
eBook (PDF) ISBN 978-1-78985-907-2

For EU product safety concerns:
IN TECH d.o.o., Prolaz Marije Krucifikse Kozulić 3, 51000 Rijeka, Croatia, info@intechopen.com or visit our website at intechopen.com.

Meet the editor

Dr. Ioannis Deliyannis is an assistant professor at the Department of Audio and Visual Arts, Ionian University, Corfu, and a founding member of Interactive Arts Research Laboratory. He has created various interactive multimedia systems ranging from experimental television stations featuring multiple modes of delivery to educational and transmedia games. He is the author of a series of journal and conference publications in the above fields and a series of books targeting the experimental and creative aspects of the technologies involved. His research focuses on the design of user-centered games and environments, and he employs sensory systems to create intelligent interactive applications, serious games and educational processes, and assistive applications for people with disabilities using technologies that include holograms with augmented and virtual reality systems.

Contents

Preface

The book addresses the topics of game design, intelligent interaction, gamification, edutainment, serious games, and mixed game modes, including the technologies that support game implementation and content delivery. The chapters address the topics of user/content requirements, documenting and evaluating the case studies that were selected. Chapters with proprietary games and technologies are also included, as they are useful to analyze particular game design and development practices followed in the industry. Today, the unification of virtual reality, augmented reality, real life with virtual gaming modes, and the use of agents or other supportive/instructional techniques is clearly a subject of high interest, including the use of artificial intelligent technologies. Other aspects of interest addressed include social intelligence applied to games, aesthetics, interaction, and usability.

I would like to thank all colleagues from the Interactive Arts Research Laboratory at Ionian University for their support in the reviewing process.

https://inarts.eu/en/lab/staff/

Dr Ioannis Deliyannis
Assistant Professor,
Department of Audio and Visual Arts,
Ionian University,
Corfu, Greece

Section 1

Design

Chapter 1

Categorizing Game Design Elements into Educational Game Design Fundamentals

Mifrah Ahmad

Abstract

Educational games have become a highly prominent tool in schools to deliver an exciting learning experience. Large amount of literature discusses the importance of how educational games are designed has been highlighted that delivering learning through educational games design and how the game designers require crucial skills to design. Educational game design requires elements which are considered during the designing process. Looking at the projection of "Game designing or the process of game design is a complex task, and it is still being investigated". Therefore, this chapter intends to discuss recent and prominent proposed game design elements that demonstrate their important characteristics in designing educational games. Consequently, two highly significant game design theorists with established fundamental elements of games are discussed. With critically understanding the elements, this chapter provides categorizing various existing game elements into established fundamental elements. Henceforth, it demonstrates a clearer overview of how game design elements can be categorized and applied. Future recommendations are also discussed.

Keywords: educational games, game design, design elements, key elements, game-based learning, fundamental

1. Introduction

Over the past decade, educational games (EG) and game-based learning (BGL) have become more common as a tool for learning and educational deliverance, as opposed to pure entertainment, which has gained immense popularity. Digital games are developed to be consumed through smartphones, computers, tablets, etc., whereas nondigital games explore the use of resources such as boards, card, pencils, and papers [1–4]. Game-based learning (GBL) is a pedagogical approach that utilizes EGs to support learning [5]. GBL utilizes an appropriate set of game mechanics (the rules of EG), provides freedom for learners to recreate scenarios without having a fear of adverse reactions, and provides a problem-oriented learning process to allow learners achieve learning goals in the EG [6].

Although the research has managed to accomplish a large range of EGs that has delivered its function successfully, there have been many EGs that have reported to be a failure or unsuccessful. It is definite that game designers do not create replicas of the games that are well-recognized. Therefore, recent articles have addressed the rise in tension between stakeholders (game designers, teachers, developers, learners, students, players) involved in designing an EG and what causes the failure. Designers are required to enhance the educational tools by integrating game elements and core concepts to maximize the tools' effectiveness, to increase the possibilities of achieving learning outcomes, levels of engagement, and motivation [7, 8]. In addition to that, designing EG requires multiple consideration of multiple stakeholders such as game designers, developers, educators, teachers, and software engineers.

Game-based learning (GBL) has been defined by identifying its principles and mechanisms [9]. The principles target intrinsic motivation, learning through "fun", authenticity (i.e. contextualized learning), self-reliance/autonomy, and experiential learning. Mechanisms include rules, clear but challenging goals, fantasy, progressive levels of difficulty, interactivity, player control, uncertainty, feedback, and a social element. This study focuses on the definition of GBL defined by Perrotta [9] as it involves game mechanics that are related to game design aspects. This may be due to a little consensus between researchers and among teachers as to how games could be used for educational purposes. GBL is specifically designed to teach specific concepts or to strengthen competencies. There exists a broad scope of games including digital and non-digital ones [1, 10–12].

Understanding the game design is a complex job. As defined, "Design is a process by which a designer creates a context to be encountered by a participant, and from which meaning emerges" [13]. Game design (GD) is defined as a variety of game design elements and learning theories that establish and define an EG. For example, design elements include goals, the game mechanism (rules), interaction, freedom, the narrative, challenges, motivational attributes, and also interactive problem-solving. Similarly, GD is equipped with learning characteristic that adds the value of providing a good learning experience to the learners. Some of the characteristics are learning outcomes, usability, user's experience, motivation, engagement, game design, user satisfaction, usefulness, understandability, performance, playability, pedagogical aspects, efficacy, social impact, cognitive behaviour, enjoyment, acceptance, and user interface [14–17]. The innovative learning approach derived from EG possesses educational values or even different kinds of software applications that compile into knowledgeable aspects such as teaching enhancement, assessments, and evaluation of learner [18].

The objective of this chapter is to comprehend game design elements that are scattered in literature for designing EGs and reflect their practicality to game design fundamentals established in prominent books by leading game designers/scholars: (1) The Art of Game Design [7]; (2) Educational Game Design Fundamentals [8]. With that, the discussion on how game design elements can be categorized and the need of reducing the duplication of elements that already exist is discussed. Therefore, this chapter attempts to provide a holistic idea based on how theoretical frameworks/models consume game design fundamentals established and how the collaboration between the designing process of EG and software design can provide a promising impression. Lastly, future direction and recommendations provide an understanding of the current approach in research for game designers, teachers, educators, and software engineers.

2. Background

As observed by leading game designers, the essence of a "game" is a problem-solving or a puzzle-solving with which competence is developed through a trial-and-error and exploration learning practice [7, 19]. Players choose from the choices they experience in real-world and learn from those actions and feedback provided by the game, leading to an interactive learning experience. EG's remarkable motivational power includes challenges that thrill and excite players, teach, and master achievements: "It is the act of solving puzzles that makes games fun. In other words, with games, learning is the drug" [19].

2.1 Recent movement through game design frameworks and models

An interesting theoretical framework for serious game design explores to integrate the "balance" between pedagogy and game design process [20]. It is comprised of play, pedagogy, and fidelity whilst discussing theoretical grounds on constructivism; however, the paper clearly demonstrates the overarching challenges faced in order to combine interdisciplinary element and the nature of the game. The complication arises when the "balancing" between elements such as skills with challenge or fidelity with pedagogy or fidelity with objectives of pedagogy and play is placed in one design process. The framework does embark towards the idea of combining multiple disciplines to provide a guideline for educators and game designers to visualize game design process based on three major elements of designing games; the framework needs to provide testing and evaluating procedures to inform how it can be used whilst the game is undergoing a process of design.

Another exciting theoretical framework for instructional design of a game was proposed as "gaming the system" [21], which consisted of structural elements and dynamics of designing a game through three (3) levels: first, micro level which describes the problem-solving or challenges faced by the player and achieving skills or learning outcomes through motivational and exploratory learning; second, macro level describing the fiction and scenarios of the game, whilst looking at enhancing learner's identity and gameplay strategies that are adopted by the learner and satisfying the motivational aspect of learning through experience; and third, metalevel that is divided into the builder and social level, focusing on contributing to game and learning design skills and social experience and social identity of players. Another study provided a conceptual framework for adapting collaborative multiplayer games by adopting the concept of multiplayer games and gameplay design principles [22]. First, it is built on an existing model of players to provide insights into the audience, and then, it develops a typology of gameplay themes to help designers with conceptualizing actions on the screen. Finally, it provides a framework with five main game design components, namely, learning objectives, story, 3D world, gameplay, and evaluation.

Recently, two highly sophisticated types of research were published on game designing. The first research proposes a hybrid theoretical framework that analyses a few existing design models, the learning theories embedded in them, and the user experience component [14]. The hybrid framework is content specialist (puts developers and designer's perspectives), contains educational goals and technological aspects required around designing a game, and provides an iterative design process throughout the stages to ensure pre-production, production, and post-production are polished and enhanced. Not only that, the model includes a pedagogical approach and learning theories. Despite an immense study conducted, it is still a work in progress, and the model needs to be verified or validated through the designers and developers to ensure its practicality, and also the genre of games is serious; hence, the confusion on understanding educational games and serious games is still ambiguous.

Another recently published work on proposing an architecture of serious game design and assessing the technology establishes through emphasizing the engaging and motivating needs of game design through knowledge of learning domain [23]. Along with that, pedagogy and game design components and their collaboration between domain content and pedagogical and playful experts lead the architecture to propose a taxonomy, representing a functional architecture for supporting the conceptual design of the game. With the help of the architecture designed, the paper reports that modification of decisions of the educational robot with affecting a game, and responding to new updates to improve games or even reusability of the educational robot with the newly designed game, is beneficial through the domain content where playful experts share the design requirements. A concern to be highlighted reducing and encapsulating experts' intellect may seem quite interesting, but allowing domain experts to focus on their definitions and knowledge and not worrying on the playful aspects of letting game designers amend aspects without having them to acquire deep knowledge of domain content seems ambiguous and requires more testing to prove the authenticity of how a game design might be retrieved.

2.2 Four basic elements through "Elemental Tetrad" by Jesse Schell

The art of game design [7], experienced in professor and game designing, discusses two major trajectories: the game design process and own advice through "the lens". The lens describes the concepts through which the design decisions are approached in terms of skill levels, mechanics, aesthetics, story, and also the technological composition in industry. With the 100 lenses unfolding the designing process for designers, the discussion of each chapter unfolds from designer to experience through the game and the player, and the effort of embedding each lens into a mind map throughout the book has provided an in-depth understanding to basics of the designing process.

For example, *Lens#32* The Meaning Choices (p. 181), understanding the choices provided to the player is sufficient or making the player feel in charge or *Lens#47* The Balance (p. 205) as a recommendation to apply with any occurring design problem; however, the decisions to fix the concepts and implement occur only by the decision of programmers. Not only those, *Lens#89* The Team (p. 380), *Lens#90* The Documentation (p. 387), and *Lens#91* The Playtesting (p. 401) all fall under a very relevant yet thoughtful concepts of game designers working on communicating and working respectfully, documenting the necessary concepts, and testing the play of the game through the player's perception. This means putting game designer's thought out of the testing and covering essentials for game designers and engaging the content for video games creatively through the design process.

Consequently, the fundamental elements of a game where game designers should focus on are formed in the beginning of the design process. With the four basic elements, each of which creates a specific experiential flow defined in **Table 1**.

To explain **Figure 1**, it is crucial to mention that there is no element developed independently. They all interrelate with each other, despite the type of game being designed. For example, when you choose a set of mechanics as crucial to your gameplay, you will need to choose technology that can support them, aesthetics that emphasize them clearly to players, and a story that allows your (sometimes strange) game mechanics to make sense to the players. Consequently, choosing mechanics that make players feel like they are in the world is related to defining aesthetics. A story with a set of events lets your aesthetics emerge at the right place and have the most impact. Like any storyteller, you will want to choose aesthetics that help reinforce the ideas of your story and technology that is best suited to the particular story that will come out of your game. The technology is essentially the medium in

#	Basic element	Definition
1	Mechanics	The mechanics of the game refer to the set of rules and procedures which regulate the players' performances to achieve the goals of the game. In fact, what differentiates between more linear entertainments (such as book, movies, etc.) and games is the element of mechanics and their vital role to complement other elements of "aesthetics", "story", and "technology"
2	Aesthetics	As the name suggests, this element is very much related to how the overall environment of the game looks. Aesthetics are considered to be an exceptionally important aspect of game design because of their direct positive correlation to the players' experience. In order to help players grasp an assured feel of the game and truly immerse in the story, a certain visual technology needs to be adopted to intensify the aesthetic features of the game
3	Story	Game story refers to a series of events and the way they unfold throughout the game. This process could be either linear and predefined or emergent and in a bifurcating manner. There exists a close relation between the game mechanics and the story, as the former can pave the way for a powerful emergence and unfolding of the events in the latter
4	Technology	Represents the set of tools, resources, and know-how needed to bring the game to life. Technology is related to any form of these elements, from crayons and duct tape used in your first prototype. It is the very medium of your game where technology aesthetic elements are implemented. Highly important for the final outcomes of the game

Table 1.
The four basic elements of games and their definition, adapted from [7].

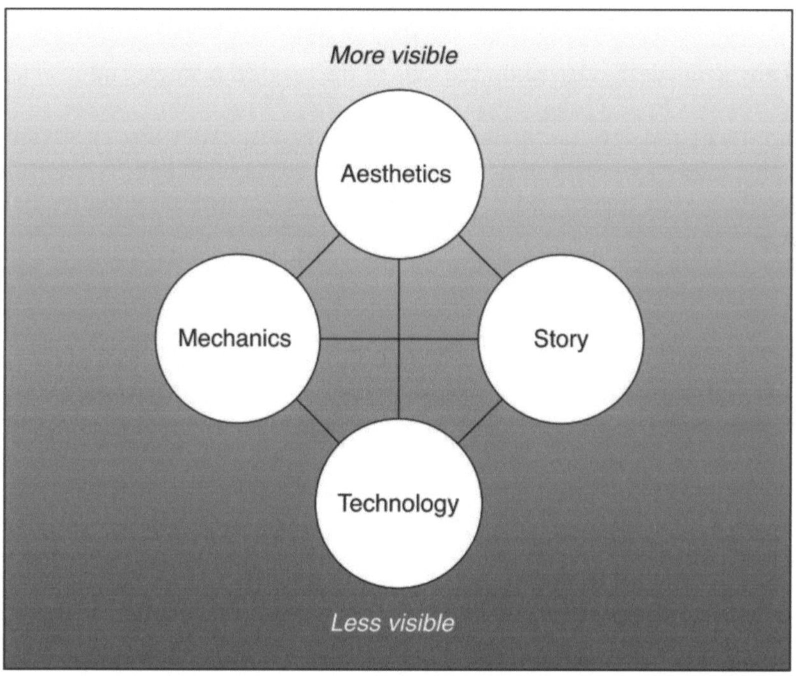

Figure 1.
The Elemental Tetrad adapted by [7].

which the aesthetics take place, in which the mechanics will occur, and through which the story will be told.

The mind map includes 30 bubbles to represent new element emerging from each chapter, and 100 lenses provided can be a very overwhelming information for the game designing team, who needs an urgent answer to the problem-solving or iterative approach. Despite the content list provided, it is noticeable to be confused with some identifications of the lens names. To conclude, a creative involvement of game systems and the player works along to endorse the experience, whilst addressing crucial organizational perspective in relevance to software development methods such as spiral model, rapid prototyping, and playtesting.

2.3 Five basic elements through "Elemental Pentad" by George Kalmpourtzis

The Educational Game Design Fundamentals by an educator, game designer, founder, director, and board member of several European design studios presents a comprehensive how-to guide on design and building world-class educational experiences [8]. It combines the evolvement, pushing through concepts and learning throughout the process by providing the reader the stand on "Games are principles and not rules" (p. 7). Although rules are elaborated on their own entirety (pp. 169–180), "rules" are illustrating that games present rules in operational constitutive and implicit way, rules present goals, and rules define ways of punishment and rewards. Kalmpourtzis highlights that game designers have the magical power to deal with challenging tasks during the educational game design process. Hence, referring to his magical triangle (p. 54), players, game, and learning aspects to structure basic elements and their relationships to create games evolve through the chapters. The emphasis on the designer's struggle to ensure that the balance is maintained in the system between the realistic and imaginative context of design is rather fruitful. Explaining that games consisted of objects and placing the objects as elements to be implemented in the game lead to the betterment of gameplay (p. 181).

"Game Core", being the most interesting establishment, discusses the concrete basis of any game design based on the axis of the magical triangle and provides three approaches to designing a game (p. 119): the unbreakable core, the flexible core, and the hybrid core. In the same context, the perspective discussed that prototyping is a key element of game design, evaluating what has been completed theoretically as well as practically. Nevertheless, Kalmpourtzis highlights that

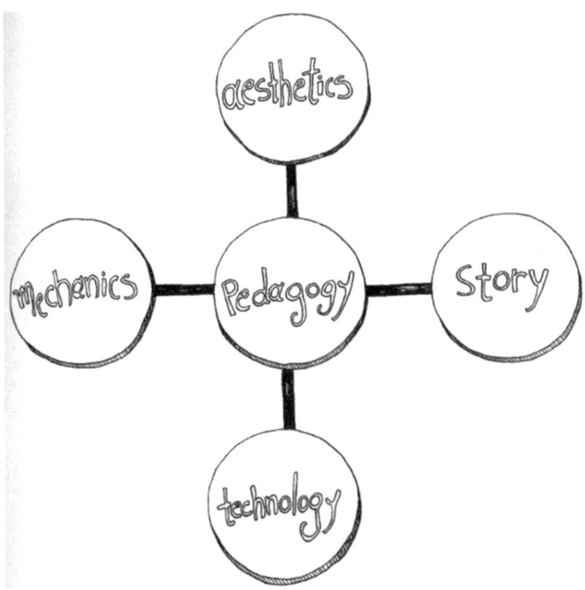

Figure 2.
A representation of the elemental Pentad adapted from [8].

interdisciplinary game design is always the most challenging aspects, i.e. an engineer working with a game designer will differ in terms of the application of the methodology to be used in building the game. Coexisting is nearly impossible in many cases, yet there is always a way to try and provide a common language as a "tool". In relation to structuring and prototyping (the fastest and easiest way), there is an evaluation of game strategies discussed which were rather general and have been published in the previous article as well [24].

The observation by Kalmpourtzis [8] understood that Schell's four basic elements collaborate and rely on each other's presence highly likely. However, Kalmpourtzis believes the need of "pedagogy" as the fifth element that is highly required in the basic fundamental elements of EG. All the elements are interrelated with learning aspects that are required to be broken down as educational game design is being implemented. He explains the crucial role of educators and their experience related to pedagogical approaches and learning theories. He examines prominent learning theories such as behaviourism, cognitivism, and constructivism. Therefore, **Figure 2** shows the extension of elemental Tetrad to Elemental Pentad.

Books	Schell [7]	Kalmpourtzis [8]
Uniqueness	**Design aspects**: • Mechanics • Aesthetic • Story • Technology **Lens # 100** – mind map for designers to unfold the design process **Games are created through**: • Playtesting • Prototyping **Documentation has a purpose** (though does not exist) (see Chapter 24): • Memory • Communication	Educational games design specific and design principles **Magical Triangle**: • Players • Game • Learning aspects **Game Cores (three of the designing processes)**: • Unbreakable • Flexible • Hybrid Common language **tool** required **Key considerations** of designing and evaluating process: Prototyping **Pedagogy** and games discussed through major learning theories: • Behaviourism • Cognitivism • Constructivism • Inquiry-based • Project-based
Difference	**Discusses:** Designer's thoughts (lens) – 100 different ways to reflect and question whilst designing the game Essential game components Engage player through experience	Discusses Schell's design aspects and adds to four elements: • Pedagogy Documentation for designing games: • Formally structured • Provides content to follow a syntax of the document
Concerns/ absence	• The mind map has 30 different points to understand which is confusing for designer's iterative work rules • Lens names are partly confusing and could be organized better • Documentation template does not exist	Author highlights: • Coexisting and interdisciplinary designing are nearly impossible • Common language "tool" required

Table 2.
Similarities, differences, and concerns noticed in the studies.

Evaluating games using usability, playtesting, and quality assurance approaches can highly coexist with software engineering approaches. Lastly, the documentation chapter (p. 325) had a new and interesting projection of how game design document shape through the designing phase, despite mentioning the difficulties faced by designers in communicating their voice formally and that the structure of the document is never the same. There are three types of documentation: the classic document (one or more documents), the wiki (online with indexed searches), and the forum (participatory process) (p. 327).

To conclude the discussion of game design fundamentals, "lens" of game design, and educational game design fundamentals and cores, **Table 2** summarizes the key movement from 2008 to 2018. This shows how the published work from game designers and theorists in the field. One prominent movement can be seen that 2008 presents a non-existing template with a slight interest in documenting the designing process, whilst in 2018 a formal structure has been proposed by Kalmpourtzis [8].

3. Recent educational game design elements

EG designed for learning is a division of both play and fun. Another author defines EGs as a melding of educational content, learning principles, and computer games [5]. Another definition by [25] in [26] defined it as a learning system, which realizes some or all components of the learning process (learning theory, gaining skills and experience, and estimation of knowledge level) in a game context. EGs have been specifically designed to teach people about a certain subject, expand concepts, reinforce development, understand historical events or cultures, or assist them in learning a skill as they play [27]. Generally, EG is a game that combines both game design principles and learning theories with the integration of learning content of the specific subject or learning outcomes purposely to enrich learning for intended audiences.

Games deliberately designed for education definitely requires some degree of effectiveness in order to be accepted by stakeholders. Researchers suggested that effective games should combine good game design and good pedagogy [28, 29]. Game design has similar concepts applied in entertainment games that should be adapted into EGs, so it can offer certain degrees of engagement as it is in entertainment games. Game design with a fun aspect includes challenges, goals, feedback, and game story. These elements derive the concepts of the game as described by various authors [30, 31]. These elements are said to be crucial in a game to really behave as a game [5, 29, 32–34]. Without those elements, games cannot really be claimed as a game, but rather similar to edutainment concepts as suggested by [35].

The explosion on game design elements in research has been clearly creating duplication of some existing elements proposed previously. This not only causes confusion but also leads to a misunderstanding of many other elements and their importance in EG. The following are a few highly prominent design elements with their definitions to demonstrate their distinctive role in games.

Table 3 shows the elements that are required for an effective video game, adapted from [10]. **Table 4** defines the core elements of a well-designed EG that enhance the design of educational games [36]. **Table 5** defines the game design factors [17]. **Table 6** shows the key elements for designing an educational video game [37].

Game design (GD) being defined and established with a variety of game design elements and learning theories in EG is explicitly mentioned in [17]. **Table 5** shows examples of game design elements that are crucial. Similarly, GD is equipped with

Elements	Definition
Edutainment	Edutainment games are those which follow a skill and drill format in which players either practice repetitive skills or rehearse memorized facts
Motivational attribute	Motivation to play is a significant characteristic of an educational video game to provide rewards. Motivation also leads to the activation of efficient cognitive strategies for long-term memory issues like monitoring, elaborating, or organizing information. On the opposite side, resignation and motivation have negative results on memorization and personal development
Goals and rules	Goals in effective video games: finding that goals of different levels help motivate learners to continue playing
Narrative context	It provides the proper context for the two processes of "learning" and "problem-solving" to take place. Providing an optimum narrative context helps players to either identify or construct patterns of cause and effect in the game through which they can connect what is "known" and what is "speculative" or "abstract" within the story [38]
Interactivity	Interaction between the player and the game environment is another element embedded in the narrative context and game objectives. The best games are "highly interactive, deliberately generating tension between the degree of control the story imposes and the player's freedom of interaction" [39]
Multisensory	"Multisensory cues can engage learners, direct their attention to important behaviours and relationships, help them understand new sensory perspectives, prevent errors through feedback cues, and enhance ease of use" [40]

Table 3.
The elements of an effective video game [10].

Elements	Definition
Interactive problem-solving	A continuous interaction between players and the game, made possible through a series of problem-solving tasks
Specific goals/rules	Incorporation of a set of rules to define the "what" and "when" of the players' actions which allow the achievement of a set of implicit or explicit goals in the game
Adaptive challenges	This is what differentiates between good games and the best games. The former maintains a balance and a comfort zone between the game challenges and the players' abilities. In the latter, the game goes one step further to introduce a challenge right at the edge of students' abilities
Control	Providing opportunities to inspire players' influence on the gameplay, the environment, and the overall learning experience
Ongoing feedback	Providing apt and relevant explicit or implicit feedback on players' performances with the purpose of improving the learning experiences' outcome
Uncertainty	Creating a sense of "suspense" and therefore provoking more player engagement with the game. A clear-cut conveyance of the game outcome will reduce the game's allure and attraction
Sensory stimuli	Refers to the interplay of the graphics, sounds, and storyline (not necessarily in a compellingly "professional" state) with the purpose of provoking players' senses

Table 4.
The seven (7) "core elements of a well-designed EG" [36].

learning characteristic that adds the value of providing a good learning experience to learners. The authors presented a macro design concepts [17] that reveal 11 crucial game design factors (**Table 6**): (1) game goals, (2) game mechanism, (3) game fantasy, (4) game value, (5) interaction, (6) freedom, (7) narrative, (8) sensation, (9) challenges, (10) sociality, and (11) mystery.

Factors	Description
Game goals	Providing the correct game experience for the players to pursue relevant goals
Game mechanism	Methods through which designers' goals are transferred to and achieved by the players to allow for a smooth operation of the virtual world
Interaction	Generation of relevant interactional and conflict feedback by the computer according to players' performances during the game
Freedom	Acknowledgement of player autonomy and agency in the game space, such as creation of avatars
Game fantasy	Game context which allows for the provision of virtual and imagery effects
Narrative	Describing event occurring in the virtual world
Sensation	Presentation of the virtual world through multimedia elements
Game value	Defined as the potential to increase players' game motivation
Challenges	Players' efforts to overcome/achieve game obstacles/goals
Sociality	Creating opportunities for interaction among players to promote communication, cooperation, competition, and/or conflict
Mystery	Maintaining a sense of curiosity and mystery through creation of novel and unique experiences

Table 5.
Eleven game design factors by [17].

Another recently published work highlighting the key elements for designing an educational video game or the crucial elements for narrative content that can enhance the educational aspect of the game are provided [37] (see **Table 6** for the definitions).

Key elements	Definition
Game structure	**Act:** much like a theatre play, act refers to each main part of the game into which the storyline is divided. There has to be at least a minimum of one act and a potential maximum **Scene:** different subdivisions of an act entailing an introduction, a plot, and a climax for each act **Action:** different subdivisions of a scene describing events in the game storyline. Each action may bear certain educational challenges **Dialogue:** any action corresponding to a conversation between game characters
Scenario	A two- or three-dimensional visual representation within which scenes can take place. There is no one-to-one relation between scenes and a scenario, so multiple scenes can occur in one scenario, or a particular scene can signify a change of scenario
Characters	Entities of the scenes performing actions and dialogues, of whom both the physical appearance and personality traits need to be designed. Normally, the player's avatar will be assigned the role of a protagonist (hero of the game). The presence or absence of the avatar can also be defined by the first-person or third-person narration of the story
Interactive objects or active parts of the scenarios	Objects of props to which some kind of functionality is allocated. These can be collected by the avatar and saved in their inventory. The assigned functionalities of the objects can later be utilized to further the purposes of the game
Educational competences	A set of skills and personal dispositions defined in a specific curricular context. For example, the Spanish Education System defines eight

Key elements	Definition
	competencies such as linguistics communicative, cultural and artistic, mathematical, etc.
Educational challenges	Challenges designed by pedagogical experts with the purpose of providing space of the development of those competences according to the proposed educational curriculum
Sounds	Includes all the acoustic features of the game: voices, effects, and music
Gameplay or the set of game rules	An underlying connection of a specific concept to a specific game genre with the purpose of regulating players' interactions with game mechanisms, which would eventually lead to the accomplishment of educational objectives, whilst maintaining a satisfactory gaming experience
Adaptation	A mechanical and instinctive adjustment of the game based on players' performance. It necessitates understanding the adjustable and configurable elements of the game by getting feedback from the players' profile, such as method of interaction, educational challenges and assessment, and the narrative.

Table 6.
Key elements for designing an educational video game [37].

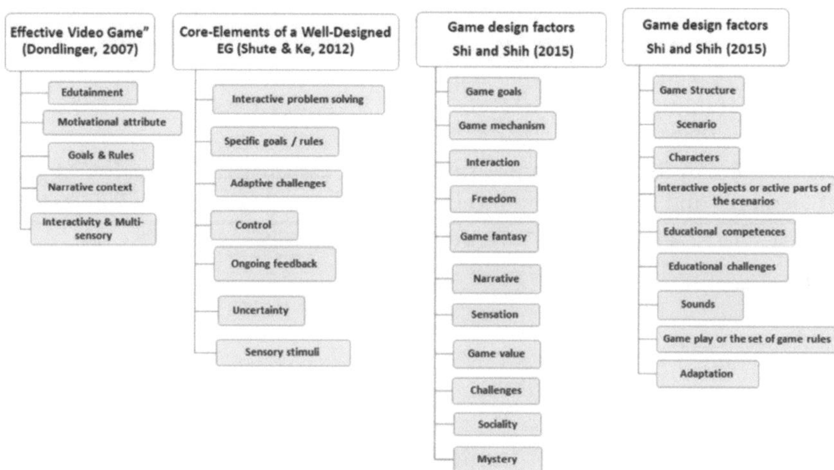

Figure 3.
Adapted from elements of an effective video game [10], core elements of well-designed games [36], game design factors [17], and key elements for designing an educational video game [37].

Figure 3 accumulates the game design elements discussed in details above. **Figure 3** is designed in this chapter to provide a clearer overview of the list of elements discussed before proceeding into grouping in Elemental Pentad.

4. Solution and recommendation

To understand the majority of game design elements and their need in designing a game is a tough task. The game design elements discussed in this chapter are understood and mapped onto the Elemental Pentad (**Figure 2**). Based on the definitions of the fundamental elements (Elemental Pentad) and the definitions of the design elements from various research, careful observation on their definitions draws onto the idea of grouping a large number of elements onto five main fundamental elements. This way, it will allow game designers to be able to distinguish the categorized elements in different key elements and the fundamentals of the game design process from the start of their process.

The elements are grouped under the five (5) main fundamental elements as shown in **Figure 4**. The elements are grouped into fundamental elements to provide a broader way of approaching the elements of educational game design as it is an entirely a challenging task. Game designers are required to have various skills where they should be able to listen and observe, knowing the fact that games are not the only solution to everything, they should be able to communicate and present their ideas through various mediums with other team members who are not game designers, and they are constantly learning. Not only that, but they are also aware of the context in which they have to integrate the learning perspective. However, their views and experience are entirely different from the views and experience a teacher or an education would preserve.

With the scattered game design elements and continuous exploration of research, the academicians are required to understand that the duplication of elements is only leading to a more confusion pattern. This chapter covers only the very prominent studies, which published elements that can provide an effective video game, or the core of an EG to be a well-designed element required a number of elements or the game design factors that need to be considered in designing an EG. The key elements for designing an EG proposed [37] provide an overview of how distinctive it is with designing a game. EGs are comprised of a fundamental element, pedagogy. Pedagogy is what seems to differentiate the game characteristics of EG vs an entertaining game. Hence, designing an educational game is not getting any easier.

With respect to that, this chapter intends to accumulate a few scattered game design elements and group them onto Elemental Pentad (**Figure 4**). The categorization provides a range of aspects to visualize a few crucial features.

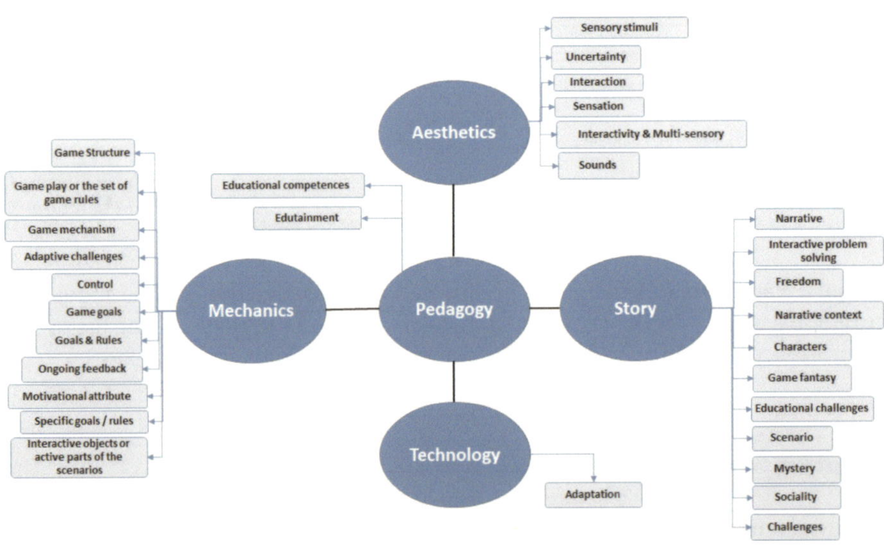

Figure 4.
A proposed categorization of game design elements onto five fundamental basic elements of an educational game.

1. Only "Key elements for designing an Educational Video Game [37]" mentioned design elements for fundamental element pedagogy.

2. Repetition of elements under fundamental element mechanics:

    a. Goals

    b. Goals and rules

    c. Specific goals/rules

3. Repitition of elements under fundamental element story:

    a. Narrative

    b. Narrative context

    c. Educational challenges

    d. Challenges

Although there still seem to be duplicate or ambiguous elements under the mechanics fundamental element, it opens a room for discussion on a few crucial matters in the research. Under the story fundamental element, the design element challenges and educational challenges seem to be repetitive. This is due to the fact that some elements are referred to as general concepts in designing a game and some are referred specifically for EG. Exploring game elements is a tedious task, and it requires a deeper understanding to why there is a duplication in elements being proposed and why the Elemental Pentad proposed is not being used to provide a definite understanding for all types of game team (stakeholders).

This now opens the research to understand that, despite an emerging range of game designing elements and models and frameworks to assist game designers, teachers, and game developers to understand the need of educational aspect, there is a need to reduce duplication, reducing the confusion of existing work and new proposed work in designing educational games. Below is the list of a few projections that can be pursued and how the researchers should be able to understand these gaps. With the understanding, there is a need to comprehend:

1. The terms used to describe games as educational game design requires a categorization.

    a. Well-designed games, effective video game, educational games, serious game?

2. The number of emerging game design elements is being produced rapidly, and hence, duplication occurs.

    a. Understanding why some researches define game designing elements as:

        i. Elements?

        ii. Factors?

iii. Key elements?

iv. Core elements?

v. Effective elements?

3. There is a need to remove or reduce duplication of design elements to avoid confusion.

4. Categorization may assist the game designers to keep on track, despite overwhelming challenges exist, including "common language" that could help communicate with the team members.

5. Stakeholders including educators, teachers, and also learners can reflect with the elements and relate their experience to ease game designing task.

5. Conclusion

This chapter discusses a few prominent game design elements published over the past decade and intends to group them onto established fundamental elements (Elemental Pentad). This is to demonstrate an easy projection on selecting the game design elements for designing process of educational games. This research will continue the grouping of elements to enhance the proposed grouping in this chapter.

Acknowledgements

This chapter contributes part of researcher's PhD study under the literature review, and the researcher would like to thank Deakin University Postgraduate Research Scholarship (DUPRS) program for giving her the opportunity to support and undertake the research.

Author details

Mifrah Ahmad
Deakin University, Melbourne, Australia

*Address all correspondence to: mifrah09@gmail.com

References

[1] Connolly T, Stansfield M, Hainey T. Towards the development of a games-based learning evaluation framework. In: Games-Based Learning Advancements for Multi-Sensory Human Computer Interfaces. 2009. pp. 251-273

[2] Serrano-Laguna Á, Manero B, Freire M, Fernández-Manjón B. A methodology for assessing the effectiveness of serious games and for inferring player learning outcomes. Multimedia Tools and Applications. 2018;**77**(2):2849-2871

[3] Azadegan A, Hauge JB, Bellotti F, Berta R, Bidarra R, Harteveld C, et al. The move beyond edutainment: Have we learnt our lessons from entertainment games? In: International Conference on Games and Learning Alliance. Springer, Cham: Springer International Publishing Switzerland; 2014. pp. 77-89

[4] Romero M. Work, games and lifelong learning in the 21st century. Procedia-Social and Behavioral Sciences. 2015;**174**:115-121

[5] Prensky M. Digital game-based learning. Computers in Entertainment (CIE). 2003;**1**(1):21

[6] Poulsen M. Chapter 5: Learning by producing. In: Poulsen M, Kober E, editors. THE GAMEiT HANDBOOK: A Framework of Game-based Learning Pedagogy. Oslo, Norway: Play Consulting; 2011. p. 87-103

[7] Schell J. The Art of Game Design: A Book of Lenses. Burlington, USA: Morgan Kaufmann Publishers; 2008

[8] Kalmpourtzis G. In: Peters AK, editor. Educational Game Design Fundamentals: A Journey to Creating Intrinsically Motivating Learning Experiences. New York: AK Peters/CRC Press; 2018

[9] Perrotta C, Featherstone G, Aston H, Houghton E. Game-Based Learning: Latest Evidence and Future Directions. Slough: NFER; 2013

[10] Dondlinger MJ. Educational video game design: A review of the literature. Journal of Applied Educational Technology. 2007;**4**(1):21-31

[11] Selwyn N. Education and 'the digital'. British Journal of Sociology of Education. 2014;**35**(1):155-164

[12] All A, Castellar EPN, Van Looy J. Assessing the effectiveness of digital game-based learning: Best practices. Computers & Education. 2016;**92-93**: 90-103

[13] Zimmerman E, Salen K. Rules of Play: Game Design Fundamentals. Cambridge, Massachusetts, London, England: The MIT Press; 2004. 670 p

[14] De Aguiar MP, Winn B, Cezarotto M, Battaiola AL, Gomes PV. Educational digital games: A theoretical framework about design models, learning theories and user experience. In: Marcus A, Wang W, editors. International Conference of Design, User Experience, and Usability: Theory and Practice DUXU. Cham, USA: Springer; 2018. pp. 165-184

[15] Wouters P, van Oostendorp H. Overview of instructional techniques to facilitate learning and motivation of serious games. In: Wouters P, Oostendorp Hv, editors. Instructional Techniques to Facilitate Learning and Motivation of Serious Games. Advances in Game-Based Learning book series (AGBL). 1st ed. Springer, Cham: Springer International Publishing Switzerland; 2017. pp. 1-16

[16] Lameras P, Arnab S, Dunwell I, Stewart C, Clarke S, Petridis P. Essential features of serious games design in higher education: Linking learning attributes to game mechanics. British Journal of Educational Technology. 2017;**48**:972-994

[17] Shi Y-R, Shih J-L. Game factors and game-based learning design model. International Journal of Computer Games Technology. 2015;**2015**:1-11

[18] Tang S, Hanneghan M. A model-driven framework to support development of serious games for game-based learning. In: Developments in E-systems Engineering. 2010. pp. 95-100

[19] Koster R. Theory of Fun for Game Design. O'Reilly Media, Inc.; 2013

[20] Rooney P. A theoretical framework for serious game design: Exploring pedagogy, play and fidelity and their implications for the design process. International Journal of Game-Based Learning (IJGBL). 2012;**2**(4):41-60

[21] Beatty ID. Gaming the system: Video games as a theoretical framework for instructional design. arXiv preprint arXiv:14016716. 2014

[22] Sinkewicz ND. A Framework for Designing Serious Games. Vancouver: University of British Columbia Library; 2015

[23] Mestadi W, Nafil K, Touahni R, Messoussi R. An assessment of serious games technology: Toward an architecture for serious games design. International Journal of Computer Games Technology. 2018;**2018**

[24] Ahmad M, Rahim LA, Osman K, Arshad NI. Chapter: 291. Towards modelling effective educational games using multi-domain framework. In: Khosrow-Pour M, DBAE, editors. Encyclopedia of Information Science and Technology. 4th ed. Hershey, PA: IGI Global; 2018. pp. 3337-3347

[25] Ogar O, Shabalina O, Davtyan A, Kizim A, editors. Mastering programming skills with the use of adaptive learning games. Joint Conference on Knowledge-Based Software Engineering JCKBSE 2014. Volgograd, Russia: Springer International Publishing Switzerland; 2014. pp. 144-155

[26] Ibrahim R, Yusoff RCM, Omar HM, Jaafar A. Students perceptions of using educational games to learn introductory programming. Computer and Information Science. 2010;**4**(1):205

[27] Singh J, Wei LL, Shanmugam M, Gunasekaran SS, Dorairaj SK, editors. Designing computer games to introduce programming to children. In: Proceeding of the 4th International Conference on Information and Multimedia, Kuala Lumpur, Malaysia. 2008

[28] Amory A, Seagram R. Educational game models: Conceptualization and evaluation. South African Journal of Higher Education. 2003;**17**(2):206-217

[29] Klopfer E, Osterweil S, Salen K. Moving Learning Games Forward: Obstacles, Opportunities and Openness (White Paper). Cambridge, MA: The Education Arcade, Massachuesetts Institute of Technology; 2009

[30] Garzotto F, editor. Investigating the educational effectiveness of multiplayer online games for children. In: Proceedings of the 6th International Conference on Interaction Design and Children; ACM. 2007

[31] Novak J. Game Development Essentials: An Introduction. Cengage Learning; 2011

[32] Grassioulet Y. A cognitive ergonomics approach to the process of

game design and development [unpublished masters thesis]; 2002

[33] Owen M. An anatomy of games. Discussion paper produced by Futurelab, Bristol. 2005. Available at: http://www.futurelab.org.uk/resources/publications_reports_articles/discussion_papers/Discussion_Paper259

[34] Sauvé L, Renaud L, Kaufman D, Marquis J-S. Distinguishing between games and simulations: A systematic review. Educational Technology & Society. 2007;**10**(3):247-256

[35] Klopfer E, Osterweil S, Groff J, Haas J. Using the technology of today, in the classroom today. The instructional power of digital games, social networking, simulations, and how teachers can leverage them. In: The Education Arcade. 2009. pp. 1-21

[36] Shute V, Ke F. Games, learning, and assessment. In: Assessment in Game-Based Learning. Springer; 2012. pp. 43-58

[37] De Lope RP, Medina-Medina N, Soldado RM, García AM, Gutiérrez-Vela FL, editors. Designing educational games: Key elements and methodological approach. In: 2017 9th International Conference on Virtual Worlds and Games for Serious Applications (VS-Games); IEEE. 2017

[38] Dickey MD, editor. Ninja looting for instructional design: The design challenges of creating a game-based learning environment. In: ACM SIGGRAPH 2006 Educators Program. ACM; 2006

[39] Swartout W, van Lent M. Making a game of system design. Communications of the ACM. 2003; **46**(7):32-39

[40] Salzman MC, Loftin RB, Dede C, McGlynn D, editors. Science Space: Lessons for designing immersive virtual realities. In: Conference Companion on Human Factors in Computing Systems. ACM; 1996

Chapter 2

Game: Experience as an Educational Tool

Zuzana Václavíková

Abstract

With a rapid growth of information and new discoveries, curricula at schools have been massively overloaded in recent years. At the same time, modern technologies, which have accelerated the learning process in many ways, cause a lack of learning through our own experience. A solution to this state can be a game as a means of linking formal and informal learning. The use of a game might be diverse: gamification of a class with simple gaming activities folded into a game story using a scoring system, comprehensive educational games based on role-playing, or using an ICT game as a tool for recognition of the area of student's interest, a tool for asking new questions, and a tool for offering the desired experience. With regard to the knowledge we have about the learning process, it is clear that experience is still the most effective way of learning, with long-lasting sustainability. So, if we offer experience in an appropriate way, we can make the entire learning and educational process more effective.

Keywords: science, education, gamification, game-based learning, eduLARP game

1. Introduction

Game—what is it? A game may take many forms and, therefore, many different definitions. A game has been a part of human culture since time immemorial, and in terms of phylogeny, it has undergone transformations of form, purpose, and style and defined the cultures. Similarly, from the point of view of ontogenesis, a game is closely linked to the child's early age as one of the most basic ways of learning. Although the game gradually changes with adolescence, it accompanies us throughout our lives and has an irreplaceable role. Many researchers have dealt with the role of a game and its importance in human life.

2. Concept of a game

Johan Huizinga, a Dutch historian and cultural theorist, highlighted the concept of a playing man in the work *Homo Ludens* [1]. He defined a game as a voluntary activity that is performed within a fixed time and space boundaries, voluntarily accepted but with unconditionally binding rules that have a goal in themselves and accompanied by a sense of tension and joy and consciousness of "another being" than "everyday life".

Roger Caillois, a French intellectual, literary critic, sociologist, writer, and philosopher who also focused on games, in his book *Man, Play and Games* [2], defined four principles of a game, which are also four principles that organise cultural life (alea, agon, mimicry, and ilinx). According to Caillois, a game is free—no one forces us to play. Furthermore, it is always separated from everyday life, it is limited by time, and because of everyday life, it represents a special time when something else happens, where different rules apply and when, for example, aggression can be discharged with impunity. A game is not productive either—there is nothing in it, even gambling is unproductive, the values in them only circulate in the circle of players, but they do not arise. A game is subordinate to the rules and, finally, it is fictitious.

To put it simply, we will understand a game as a formal rule-based system in which the player makes an effort to influence the outcome. Because the definition of the game is very universal, it is understandable that there are a number of game classifications and different game typologies. Some sources divide the game into almost 80 categories by number of players, relation between the game and player and between the game and the outside world, or with regard to the fact whether the game is competitive, strategic, sports, computer, social, etc. In most cases, it is not important to specifically classify a game, and it often happens that a game overlaps several categories; therefore, we will not deal with it.

Besides the fact that a game is absolutely natural to us, we often have several other reasons to enjoy it. Sometimes we just need to completely clear our mind to allow our brain to refresh itself and recalibrate all of its functions (we look for simple routine games, often sports games), or we need to escape the everyday reality and we want to be someone else (we look for RPG games or strategy games), we want company or we want to be alone (looking for collective games or single-player games), etc. A game will also allow us to experience a story virtually, to try out other roles, to restructure social hierarchy. Many of today's games will give us space to participate in the process of creating the story. We can test what it would be like to "do something" with the knowledge of safety that our action will not have consequences. The main rule of every game is what happens in the game stays in the game environment, with no real consequences.

3. Learning, memory, and education

The vital importance of learning is that it enables living organisms to adapt to changing conditions of the material and social environment. All living organisms learn, from the first to the last day of life, in all environments (in different ways and things). Human learning is a relatively permanent change in a person's knowledge or behaviour due to experience [3, 4].

The concept of learning in psychology refers to the process in which changes in behaviour, mental, and personality occur in a person, through new knowledge, new skills, and mainly through experience. As a result of the learning process at the psychological level, there are not only newly acquired information, opinions, and new patterns of behaviour but also changes in emotional experience, changes in cognitive processes (e.g., in the way of perception and thinking), changes in personality traits (e.g., self-concept, motivation, moral qualities, abilities, skills, etc.), and changes in relationships with other people. Changes that occur during the life of a person in his/her psyche, personality, and behaviour are the results of the simultaneous action of both major development processes: biological maturation and learning. Moreover, maturation and learning are a dialectical relationship, interacting and conditioning each other [3–9].

Memory processes, as one of the cognitive processes, are often divided into three phases: encoding, storage, and retrieval. During storage, the brain does not store the received information in the same way (even the same kind of information). The way it is stored is likely to be determined by the type of information and its importance to the individual's life. The importance of information is probably judged by the brain according to the following:

- Attention that is given to information and interest that the information has generated. We pay more attention to information that is vital or of great interest to us.

- Emotional reaction that has been activated by information. More attention is given to information that impresses our emotions and is considered more important.

- Repetition, frequency of occurrence of information (or activity).

These findings can be used to increase the learning efficiency by deliberately inducing attention, emotional engagement, and repetition [4, 6–9].

Education is usually defined as the process of receiving or giving systematic instruction, especially at a school or university. Although education and learning are closely intertwined, the basic difference is that while learning is about the person itself, education is connected with other people—usually a teacher and a learner are needed. Any scientific approach we tend to, we can say that education has always been and will always be the synthesis of several entities—school, family, institution of informal education, and society as well. By formal education, we mean a systematic intentional way provided by a trained teacher. Informal education is the part outside the formal education and is realised in a family, peer group, by mass media, and by institution of informal education (museum, library, science centre, etc.) [10].

4. Digital generation and experience

People learn unconsciously through work, art, language, culture, and experience. The whole communication between human beings is educational. However, it should be pointed out that while in the first half of the twentieth century, learning by experience was part of everyday life—children had to engage in everyday activities around the house and in the garden—nowadays the situation is completely different, maybe scary. The so-called X generation has encountered the coming of digital technology. This technological advancement has greatly simplified people's everyday lives—many activities no longer have to be done, and thus they have not been taught anymore. Consequently the next generations, such as Y and Z, usually have no chance to learn these activities, from home after all. In parallel, the rules of some school activities have been tightened for safety reasons, especially the ones that are connected with getting experience. For example, there has been a decrease in experiments in chemistry lessons, technical work has been abolished in the school curriculum, the rules for teaching outside the school building have been restricted, etc. Everything needs to be fast, clean, and safe. The increasing age of mothers (as well as the first-time mothers) also contributed to the fact that we consider the best option when the child does nothing and goes nowhere (to avoid danger and to be safe). Safety at first: better than to risk is to do nothing. But how will the children get experience?

On the other hand, with the increase in scientific knowledge across all areas, the curriculum has become overfilled. Teachers are forced to teach quantity instead of quality in school, especially in the case of natural science subjects. There is no time for discussion, no time for experiments, and no time for explanation. And as the consequence of these changes, currently, there is no room for gaining experience. Children's natural desire to discover new things is not developed and is not supported. If there is no possibility at school, it is necessary to take advantage of afternoon time, and if we want to ensure safety, we can do it in a controlled way. So the children's free is a space for a game as a tool to offer experience, especially space for an educational game as a tool to offer controlled and safe activity with experience and educational context.

5. Educational game

Each game carries some lesson learned and shapes us somehow. A game that is explicitly designed for educational purposes is called an educational game. Usually, the goal of an educational game is to help understand concepts, learn domain knowledge, and develop problem-solving skills by playing a game. If a game is used to enhance the learning experience, we talk about game-based learning. Sometimes, we use game elements in a non-game situation—it is called gamification (e.g., corporate reward programmes based on a scoring system).

There are many games that are used at schools as a means of strengthening relationships, motor skills, and ideas or functioning in the classroom. In our context, an educational game represents a game that educates a pupil in a concrete topic or topics, usually concerning science subjects. Unlike general games, where the most important factor is a high positive emotional experience, educational games are mainly focused on the range of information offered. But we have to be careful; sometimes, in an effort to get the most educational content into a game, we offer something called a "game" but not attractive to the player. In fact, if a game is well prepared, the player should not even feel that he/she is being educated.

5.1 Review

Although the game has been accompanying us since the beginning of civilization, at the turn of the millennium, thanks to the incredibly fast development of technology, a game has come to the spotlights of scientists from many areas. Moreover, the facts on youth's consumption of digital games as well as the statistics on how much time youth spend playing digital games cause that the vast majority of studies concern digital games. Digital games are studied as a tool with a concrete purpose and goal, especially by computer designers, psychologists and neurologists, and last but not least, by educators and teachers. The main reason for starting the study of a game as an educational tool in parallel with the growth of technology was the crisis of the paradigms and educational models at the end of the twentieth century. With many benefits and high effectiveness, serious games have become a new educational paradigm. Game-based learning, together with inquiry-based learning, is currently one of the most studied teaching methods [11, 12]. Whitton [13] provides an overview of the field of digital games and learning from a cross-disciplinary perspective and describes games as active learning environments, as motivational tools, as playgrounds, as well as games as learning technology. The link between the videogames and learning, including game design, game culture, and games as a tool for teaching and learning, is described in [14] by the most influential personalities in the field. Opinions on the potential benefits of gaming on students' academic achievements, motivation, and skills in science courses are compared in review [15] to investigate the effects of using educational computer games in teaching science at the elementary education level. The state of research on the so-called role-playing games across disciplines, cultures, and media offers, for example, [16], and some concrete experience can be found in [17].

Apart from the research work, a number of web environments deal with this topic. Digital educational games for different age groups of pupils categorised by topic and curriculum can be found there for free download. Their quality varies, and it is good to carefully check the game first—scientifically and didactically—and also the game process itself. Unfortunately, they usually do not contain information for teachers about how and when to use the game, how to proceed the final analysis of achieved learning objectives, etc. There are also professional educational games, such as Minecraft: Education Edition ([18], based on the commercially successful Minecraft game). These kinds of games are of higher quality and offer methodology for teachers but are not free.

5.2 Theatre play in education

The first and the most used games in education (from the point of phylogeny as well as the ontogenesis) is role-playing, a type of mimicry game, where we play someone else. It is understandable because imitating someone and playing something are a natural part of learning. Depending on the depth of identification, role-playing has several levels—from simulation, through alternation to characterisation. Sometimes, theatre plays are denoted as role-playing games. However, it is important to realise that it depends on the extent to which the character's behaviour, speaking, and storyline are predetermined. In any case, theatre plays have played an important role in education. In this context, it is necessary to mention John Amos Comenius as one of the greatest philosophers who highlighted the potential of theatre game in the teaching process. Playing in the form of theatre was emphasised in his book *Schola Ludus* (School by Play, in 1630). Comenius used and explored the scenic play as a means of a teaching tool; he defined the didactic theatre play and included it in his own education system. He was not the first who introduced the theatre to schools; the roots date back to the fifteenth century (Roman Academy) [19]. Although it was very progressive to play theatre in the classroom, *Schola Ludus* was merely a means of rehearsing and repeating the encyclopaedic, knowledge-based material, and even where there was room for dramatisation, it was not applied. So he did not perceive a game in the present sense—as a free and creative activity.

5.3 Live action role-playing

In the second half of the twentieth century, the role-playing method began to diverge from passive imitation and staging of prescribed scenarios to be more about the role itself in interacting with others. Gradually, theatrical performance, which had its audience, started to be "live action" role-play (the so-called LARP), which is played for the purpose of the experience of the players themselves without audience. There is no prescribed scenario; the story is shaped by individual interaction roles and, therefore, develops differently within the set rules. LARP is usually performed in an authentic environment; actors have costumes, scenery, and predetermined rules. Naturally, LARPs appeared before they were scientifically defined—for example, oldies party, reconstruction of famous events (Napoleonic Wars, American Civil War), or various fans' meetings inspired by successful books or films, such as Harry Potter Star Wars, etc. LARP has proven to be also a method suitable as a team-building activity in the form of the so-called escape games. The idea of using a LARP game in the education process is eduLARP. The primary target of eduLARP is to teach students something new. EduLARP includes social interactions between pupils and interaction with the environment, too. Playing roles will allow game participants to do things they would not normally do (due to familiar conventions, fear, or little self-confidence). That is why eduLARP can develop soft skills as a secondary goal. Additionally, the location of the topic of eduLARP in space and time offers a wide range of inter-subject linkages. Lots of eduLARPs are focused on history or science subjects like chemistry, physics, biology, etc.

Although there exist schools that have a whole school curriculum based on eduLARP (e.g. Østerskov Efterskole, [20]), probably it cannot be applied to the majority of schools. However, there is a great potential precisely in the possibility of spontaneous interconnection of formal and non-formal education and the use of free afternoon time of pupils, because even one interesting game can start to evoke interest in seeking answers. The research shows that eduLARPs are very popular and really work in educational sense [21, 22].

5.4 Science education games

In the context of a game in natural science subjects, it is welcome to use a game in every situation where possible—from small, simple games in the lessons, to complex gamification of the classroom. By using a good game, we are able to target the increase of attention, evoke emotion, or ensure repetition and moreover, consequently, ensure that information is necessary to be stored and saved in our brain.

There are several most used kinds of games in the educational process. The first ones are short, fast, and easy games, usually used at the beginning of the lesson as a start-up game (recall of the topic). However, they are not too emotionally charged, and, therefore, the effect of these games is more in the deepening of the importance of the information for our brain by frequent repetition of the activity. They can also be used in students' free time, but for their unattractiveness they are not much sought after.

Role-playing games are more action-packed and more emotional for pupils. They bring better educational effect, and stronger emotional engagement in the game will make it easier to remember the experience. However, their preparation and implementation are very demanding both financially and in time. Schools mostly use the offer of institutions of informal education [23]. These games are very popular, but they are one-time. Often, the initial enthusiasm fades away, and the educational benefit is not further developed.

Therefore, year-round games are now being developed through gamification of the classroom, based on role-playing. By meaningfully implementing short games and sub-activities into a story that runs throughout the school year, and by using a scoring system, we can motivate pupils to be active the whole year. As part of the story, pupils have to face the challenges, and by solving them they get points that move them forward in the story. The benefit is also that pupils do most of these partial activities in the afternoon, combining them with a discussion at school. The teacher does not have to spend too much time by playing the game at school. It is enough to inspire the children to play the game in their free time and to confront the success and result of the game in the class with the teacher and classmates.

6. Design of an educational game

6.1 Features of an educational game

It is absolutely crucial for the educational effect that a review analysis follows the game. It means discussing with the pupils the progress of the game, key moments, and feelings of the game. As part of this discussion, the teacher explains the educational passages—the students' approaches of solving are compared, or the teacher can show other solutions. By discussing how and why a player has decided in a given way and what the decision has led to, we gain more experience. We can compare our point of view with the views of other players, often realising that we missed some information in the game and our opinion was wrong. Often, the game gives us a chance to introduce some other, secondary topics that could be in the interest of the players and raise new questions. In the framework of the review analysis, there is also room for discussing these open questions. The teacher can encourage pupils to focus on some new topics, show them why these topics are interesting, and guide them on how and where they can get more information. Finally, the most important thing is to tell the students what was real and what was fiction in the game. Of course, the learning goal is carried out by the game itself, but its effect may be increased several times by the final review analysis.

The second thing, but not less important, is that phenomena and processes must work in the game the same way as they do in real life. Or at least they should work by the same way as they are in the model explained in the corresponding curriculum. Different or general models can then be discussed in the review analysis. The teacher can explain to the pupils what other phenomena affect the process.

For example, in one-escape game, themed on a sinking ship's escape, the first announcement to the players was that the key from the emergency exit door was hidden carefully. The aim of the game was then to find, through the sequence of indications, the safe in which the key was stored and the combination of numbers to open the lock. The game was pretty well done except for the basic one—a big mistake. Everybody knows that an emergency exit must be always clearly marked—it is a way to save life. So why should the key be hidden? Then, if the players were not successful in the first few steps, they stopped to be interested in the game because, quite understandable, they felt it as stupid.

It is important for players to be able to draw on their own experience. The game teaches us to adapt to another environment and teaches us how to make the right decisions. It is implemented through showing us what reaction our action will cause. By monitoring the consequences of our activity, we can then improve and accelerate our decisions. However, if the game behaves differently than our experience shows, it will cause confusion in our thinking.

In some cases, the game may be placed in a fictitious environment where some mechanisms work differently. In this case, it must be clearly explained and justified to the players in advance.

Because, as already said, individual's learning is closely linked to biological maturation, it is very important that the game be played by an individual of the age group for which the game was designed. Moreover, in an educational game, we directly follow the curriculum for the target group, and we know in advance what the player already knows and what we want to teach them.

Even a perfect game, if played at a disproportionate age, can have a negative influence, because the child did not sufficiently mature for the game. Not only the game can be difficult or incomprehensible to them, but the emotional experience may not be correctly absorbed and understood. Therefore, it is really important to choose games carefully and follow the target group the game is intended for.

6.2 Form of the game

There is a wide range of different games in offer. If we want to use a game in education, we have two options—to use existing games or to create something of our own. The advantage of the first option is definitely timesaving and high quality if we choose good games. The disadvantage is that it is very difficult to orientate in the game offer, and it is not always easy to choose the game for the purpose we need. On a didactic platform, discussions about which games are suitable for educational purposes are often restricted to two basic questions:

- The first is whether to select digital/computer games or non-digital/non-computer games.

- And the second, whether individual/single-player games, multiplayer games, or team games are more appropriate.

Discussions on the first question are diverse—from the opinion that computer games are best to the opinion that they are completely inappropriate. It must be emphasised that we live in the digital era and whether we like it or not, digital technologies have become part of everything we do. So targeted repression of digital games is not good. It is also important to realise that every game, whether computer or non-computer, has both positives and negatives. Usually, computer games allow you to play anywhere, anytime. It offers us the opportunity to communicate online with anyone in the world, giving us the possibility of distant friendships with people of the same interests. It also offers to play with a different identity in an impersonal collective, i.e., without prejudice. But even though the game is well graphically processed and accompanied by sound, the experience is not as strong as when a player is in a real environment, where they also feel touch, fear, delight, coldness, etc. On the contrary, games, where real face-to-face contact of the player takes place, are better from the point of improving social behaviour. They build more personal relationships, players do not tend to behave too extremely, and experiences (especially social) are more felt. This approach of a game also transfers the existing relationships between the classmates to the game. This fact can have a positive as well as a negative effect. Sometimes, it happens that pupils who are rivals in real life are unable to cooperate in the game, or at least they try to take revenge on each other during the game.

Comparing the advantages and disadvantages of a computer and non-computer game, the best solution is to combine both approaches. In a face-to-face contact-based game, digital technology passages should be implemented.

The answer to whether individual or team games, single-player or multiplayer (cooperating or competing) games, are more appropriate is analogous. Both types have their advantages and disadvantages, and it is good to combine both. The advantage of individual or single-player games is that the player does not depend on the time possibilities of others. Furthermore, the game results uniquely reflect the pupil's competences, and the teacher sees how the student has improved within their own knowledge and skills.

Team games, in addition to strengthening relationships between pupils, reflect real life. We are usually dependent on someone and forced to cooperate. Moreover, if a game is well designed, everyone can offer their own skills to the team. In team, there is a place for making use of the talent and abilities of each student to its full extent and in the field which is dominant for each student. If each student can offer the best and will see that it is valuable for the whole team, the game will be interesting for everyone.

This case opens the question about the division of students into teams. It can be based on their friendships or determined by the teacher. The first case is more natural, but the teams may be unbalanced in the sense of knowledge and skills. In the second case, it could happen that students in the team will not cooperate.

In gamification, the model of alternating individual work and teamwork is often used.

7. Our experience with preparing games

7.1 Study modules: creative science

The first educational activities, based on some kind of a game and focused on bringing in real experience, were started to be offered in 2009 as part of educational programmes in the science centre—The World of Technology Ostrava [24]. We realised the Inventor class under the licence of the Netherlands Kids and Science Foundation, and, at the same time, we started to design the study modules of creative science. Creative science is a 3-hour module for pupils focused on creative production of various devices, physical or mathematical "toys", from commonly available materials which can be tried either at home or at school [25, 26].

7.2 EduLARPs

Our experience with the first eduLARP began in 2013. We offered the eduLARP game Odyssea Holy, focused on inorganic chemistry, for students aged 15–18, in the form of one-day activity for schools. The game was provided at the science centre and was guided by specially trained animators who formed part of the story. Initially, it was only a pilot programme, but from the first moment eduLARPs were already in great demand. Currently, there are three eduLARP games in offer, played in the science centre.

In view of the great interest, there was an idea of creating an eduLARP game that could be played in schools without the need of animators, guided only by teachers, based on a pre-studied game scenario and accompanying methodology. Therefore, in 2017, we started to develop eduLARP games that could be downloaded, pre-studied, and played at any school without the assistance of an external subject. Part of the game description is a methodology for teachers and animators, apps to download if used, animations, presentations, and all the necessary materials in a printable format. There are four games designed for 10–15-year-old students, and the primary educational content is mathematical, with other science subjects appearing secondarily. The games were created in cooperation with LARPists (designers and players of general LARP games) and scientific experts, didactics, and methodologists, who ensured the correctness and adequacy of the educational content. These games are also available for download in the English language [27].

7.3 Gamification of a classroom

In parallel with LARPs, in 2016, we started to work on the creation of a year-round game focused on natural sciences. The game is implemented through the gamification of a classroom, using the scoring system. It is designed for lower secondary school students (ISCED 2A), and the science curriculum is intermingled by mathematics. The main storyline has been prepared, and partial activities have been designed, which we also wanted to connect with the region—information about the history of the town and information about various cultural attractions are also included.

A great advantage of this year-round game is also the fact that it is possible to incorporate there what ordinary life no longer offers, or what we do not want to accept much in everyday life. A typical example is patience—today's generation is already used to having everything right now. However, many things cannot be rushed, and we often need to teach children to be patient. These requirements can be incorporated into the year-round game by including activities that cannot be accelerated in time. For example, in our year-round game, one challenge is that the pupil gets three seeds of an unknown plant during the game and the next indicia can be an exchange for a grown-up plant. Therefore, they must try to successfully cultivate at least one of the three seeds. This process cannot be accelerated, and if it fails, they must try to get new seeds passing the side storyline.

Some partial activities have been already pilot-verified and are now being finalised with the design of the whole game. Subsequently, it will be necessary to pilot the whole game and modify the disputed parts.

7.4 Game as a recognition tool

All of the above-mentioned games were primarily designed as non-computer, face-to-face games, with digital technology only as a sub-tool used in the game (most often apps for some specific tasks). For school children, we considered contact games more appropriate. A disadvantage which we have not mentioned yet is that after playing the game, it is difficult to return to the passages or key moments of the game, even during the subsequent review analysis. Sometimes pupils disagree with each other how certain events have gone—and it is not possible to find the truth, because the game is not recorded. It may not be important for the effect of the game itself, but it could be helpful for the teacher who wants to understand the behaviour and the way of deciding by individual pupils. This, on the other hand, is completely unproblematic for computer games, because data can be easily loaded and saved. With regard to the fact that inclusion in education is currently being applied at schools, there is an issue that teachers are not able to identify individual pupils' needs and identification tools are relatively lengthy with often vague results. We have started to think about the possibility of using the game to find out something about the way of students' thinking. The most problematic is the identification of gifted and twice-exceptional students (i.e., gifted children who give evidence of one or more disabilities—like SpLD, ADHD, speech and language disorder, etc.).

We are interested only in natural science talent (not a sport, art, and music talent), so we are focused on skills like decision-making, problem-solving, logical thinking, strategic thinking, and creativity. We are working on a design of the game that could be the tool for the nomination of gifted pupils. Such a game could help the teacher better understand pupil's thoughts and realise that, for example, a seemingly disobedient pupil could be talented and looks like undisciplined because of being bored in the class. Through the game, we will be able to find out the area of interest of students, and we can offer the players to develop and improve their knowledge.

8. Conclusion

Free time of children, which was once naturally filled with learning through experience, is becoming unused. Nowadays, afternoon free time is mostly filled by a game (in majority by a computer/digital game), chosen by the child, often based on marketing pressures or from the point of popularity and attractiveness. Gradually, it will become increasingly important to use children's afternoon time more functionally for educational purposes, and it will be necessary to start offering them experiences that the present time does not allow to experience naturally. A well-chosen game, adequate to the age of the player, can use this time to bring not only fun and relaxation but also learning and improving knowledge and skills. A game can also become a teachers' tool to better understand their pupils' thoughts and decision-making processes, a tool for the nomination of talented pupils, and a tool for specifying pupils' areas of interest.

DOI: http://dx.doi.org/10.5772/intechopen.88853

Currently we want to orientate further research on developing a digital game that would get us more information about the process of thinking and solving natural science problems of primary and lower secondary school pupils. In cooperation with psychologists and sociologists, we are designing the definite structure of the game, a sequence of changing states and embedded narrative elements and discussing a possibility of emergent story elements, partial tasks and questions, and optional help in the game so that we will be able to recognise the strategy of each pupil and her/his preferences from the data obtained by playing.

Author details

Zuzana Václavíková
University of Ostrava, Ostrava, Czech Republic

*Address all correspondence to: zuzana.vaclavikova@osu.cz

References

[1] Huizinga J. Homo Ludens: A Study of the Play-Element in Culture. New York: Angelico Press; 2016. 220 p. Reprint

[2] Caillois R. Man, Play, and Games. Urbana, Ill: University of Illinois Press; 2001. 208 p

[3] Ormrod J. Human Learning. 6th ed. Boston: Pearson; 2012. 624 p

[4] Collins S. Neuroscience for Learning and Development: How to Apply Neuroscience and Psychology for Improved Learning and Training. London UK: Kogan Page; 2016. 232 p

[5] Coch D, Fischer KW, Dawson G, editors. Human Behavior, Learning, and the Developing Brain: Normal Development. 2nd ed. New York: Guilford; 2007. 412 p

[6] Eysenck MW. Psychology: An International Perspective. 1st ed. New York: Psychology Press; 2004. 992 p

[7] Berliner DC, Calfee RC. Handbook of Educational Psychology. Mahwah, New Jersey: Lawrence Erlbaum Associates; 2004. 1071 p

[8] Kesner RP, Martinez JL. Neurobiology of Learning and Memory. Amsterdam: Academic Press; 2007. 473 p

[9] Bresciani M. J. The neuroscience of learning and development: Enhancing creativity, compassion, critical thinking, and peace in higher education. Stylus Publishing; 2016. 376 p

[10] Václavíková Z. Interactivity – How to Prepare Study Module. Entertainment-Education in Science Education. Kraków: Pedagogical University of Cracow; 2017. pp. 97-108

[11] Plass JL, Homer BD, Kinzer Ch K. Foundations of game-based learning. Educational Psychologist. 2015;**50**(4):258-283

[12] Kim S, Song S, Lockee B, Burton J. Gamification in Learning and Education, Enjoy Learning Like Gaming. Cham: Springer; 2018. 159 p

[13] Whitton N. Digital Games and Learning: Research and Theory. New York: Routledge; 2014

[14] Squire K, Barab S. Games, Learning, and Society: Learning and Meaning in the Digital Age. Cambridge: Cambridge University Press; 2012. 464 p

[15] Hussein MH, Ow SH, Loh SCH, Thong MK, Ebrahim NA. Effects of digital game-based learning on elementary science learning: A systematic review. IEEE Access. 2019;7:62465-62478

[16] Deterding S, Zagal J. Role-Playing Game Studies. Transmedia Foundations. New York: Routledge; 2018. 484 p

[17] Bowman SL, editor. Wyrd Con Companion Book 2014. Los Angeles, CA: Wyrd Con; 2014. 160 p

[18] Minecraft Education Edition [Internet]. Available from: https://education.minecraft.net/ [Accessed: 26 July 2019]

[19] O'Toole J, Stinson M, Moore T. Drama and Curriculum: A Giant at the Door. New York: Springer; 2010. 222 p

[20] Østerskov Efterskole [Internet]. Available from: https://osterskov.dk/in-english/ [Accessed: 03 July 2019]

[21] Hyltoft M. The role-players' school: Østerskov Efterskole. In: Montola M, Stenros J, editors. Playground Worlds: Creating and Evaluating Experiences of Role-Playing

Games. Finland: Ropeconry; 2008. pp. 232-247

[22] Hyltoft M. Four reasons why edu-larp works. In: Dombrowski K, editor. LARP: Einblicke. Braunschweig, Germany: Zauberfeder Ltd; 2010. pp. 43-57

[23] Václavíková Z. Gamification and game-based learning – How to implement them into education. In: 16th Conference of Applied Mathematics: Proceedings, Bratislava: Spektrum STU Bratislava. 2017. pp. 1592-1597

[24] Science and Technology Centre Ostrava [Internet]. Available from: http://www.stcostrava.cz/web/guest/hlavni-stranka [Accessed: 03 July 2019]

[25] Václavíková Z. Science education – Formal versus informal education. In: New Challenges in Education. Ružomberok: Verbum; 2013. pp. 260-277

[26] Václavíková Z. Creative science – The way how to improve the knowledge and skills of children. In: Mathematica V. 1st ed. Ružomberok: Verbum; 2015. pp. 91-96

[27] EduLARPs [Internet]. Available from: https://www.eduludus.cz/matematicke-edularpy/ [Accessed: 03 July 2019]

Chapter 3

Gamifying Project Procurement for Better Goal Incorporation

Maksims Kornevs, Jannicke Baalsrud Hauge and Sebastiaan Meijer

Abstract

Many services that we use daily, like healthcare, infrastructures, public transport, education, and others, are provided by the public sector. These services are provided using the project procurement process. In most cases, this process has a highly complex and dynamic interaction. It leads to issues, such as information asymmetry, over-specified tenders, not efficient feedback loops, etc. As a result, projects can rarely match to the objectives of organizations. This work explores the use of participatory simulation to help holistically investigate a project procurement process to incorporate better goals of organizations. Based on case studies from the Swedish road construction field, it can be concluded that participatory simulation is an effective approach to experiment with the effects of project procurement.

Keywords: project procurement, challenges in procurement, participatory simulation, road construction

1. Introduction

Governmental procurement is a process of obtaining goods or services. Procurement accounts for approximately 12% of the gross domestic product (GDP) of developed countries and 16% of the GDP of the European Union [1]. The purpose of the procurement is to stimulate an open market and to provide the best price for the ordered product, works, or services [2]. However, in practice, a procurement process, especially procurement that is a part of projects, can rarely match objectives of organizations [3, 4] because of technical specifications and dependencies on multiple stakeholders that are involved.

Despite the importance of procurement in a business, little work has focused on how changes and adaptations to the procurement process affect the total outcome of the system. Most of the existing studies decompose contracts into smaller, more tractable problems, such as ordering amounts in supply chain management [5]. However, such an approach cannot address the important aspect of agency and complexity in the decision-making process within procurement. To simulate a holistic view of contracts, business models, and decisions, there is a need to develop a different approach that would be able to grasp the complexity in procurement process [6, 7].

In order to achieve this, we suggest to use a participatory simulation to explore to what extent participatory simulation approach may be used for investigation of different issues existing in road project procurement and to evaluate complexity in procurement.

This study is important for several reasons. First, analysis of project procurement on different levels of planning helps to reveal the underlying issues that prevent organizations to maximize the effectiveness of the procurement process. Second, evaluating current methods allows seeing strengths and weaknesses in different methods and helps to use the advantages of participatory simulation to solve these issues. Third, the presented case studies and analysis of their results illustrates how to introduce an approach helps to grip on project procurement.

With the need to change and adapt to new regulations and norms to increase the level of innovation in such systems, there is a need to simulate the procurement process [8, 9]. Models in traditional methods of the simulation are based on close systems where choices of agents are limited. Because of that, these traditional methods do not address the important aspect of agency and complexity in the decision-making process within procurement or they try to decompose contracts into smaller, more tractable problems, such as ordering amounts in supply chain management [5]. To simulate a holistic view of contracts, business models, and decisions, there is a need to develop different simulation approaches, such as participatory simulations [7].

The chapter is organized as follows: in Section 2, we provide a background on project procurement with some common challenges and methods that are traditionally used to address some of these challenges. Section 3 describes a participatory simulation approach and how it can be applied to project procurement. In Section 4, we describe two case studies based on participatory simulation and outcomes from these studies. Finally, we conclude the paper in Section 5.

2. Background

2.1 Project procurement

Procurement is a procedure that governmental institutions need to follow in order to buy goods, services, or work over a predefined threshold. The procurement process comprises several steps [10, 11]. It starts by defining the needs and developing technical and functional specifications. Then the criteria for participation in bidding process and award criteria are specified before the documents are published. Interested companies can submit their offers or tenders. The tender that meets all the requirements and has the best offer based on the award criteria is awarded.

Although procurement is well defined on many levels, the procedure still leaves room for making decisions. Project procurement is a type of procurement that is performed as a part of a project to obtain a customized item or service. Such procurement procedures are known as project procurement.

Project procurement is used when there are no off-the-shelf solutions or products [12]. Such items or services often are required in construction projects, product development projects, information system/information technology projects, energy or hydro projects, and maintenance projects [12]. However, a majority of the project procurements are in a road construction sector [13, 14].

Road construction and maintenance are performed by a number of stakeholders with each having its own responsibilities and functions. The main stakeholder is usually a public road administration, which is a governmental organization. They have the responsibility of carrying out projects that typically require road-related works for a period of time from several years to 15–20 years [15]. This makes the procurement stage important since at this stage all works and services that will be performed in the frame of a project are defined.

2.2 Procurement at three levels of planning

Today, the major focus in procurement is on the process from the definition of the requirements for awarding the contract to the winning contractor at the end of the procurement service. However, it is important to view the role of procurement for the organization and to see how procurement fits into the "bigger picture" of an organization and how procurement is managed and planned by the organization. Often, these management tasks can be viewed by three levels of planning: strategic, tactical, and operational [16].

2.2.1 Procurement at a strategic level

The strategic level of planning includes long-term decision-making. It looks at product and process management from a life cycle point of view. In business, project procurement can be seen at a strategic level, when all or most of the project executions are procured and developed by other companies [17].

For example, in the architectural, construction, and manufacturing industries, products or works can be obtained as design-build contracts. In this case, a client is paying for a design, building, or manufacturing and supporting the product or work. It gives more freedom for bidders to look at the product in a holistic way and make improvements from the life cycle perspective [18]. However, it reduces the control level of a client and can create more risks in cases when the company that won the tender does not fulfill all obligations [19].

2.2.2 Procurement at a tactical level

Tactical level focuses on demands and achieving the best end value. Most procurement contracts are made at this level based on best practices and experience of an organization [20].

Usually, procurement at the tactical level is carried out for products or services for an extensive period of time (from 1 to 7–8 years depending on the field) [21]. A big part of the procurement process is done based on existing templates and established guidelines.

2.2.3 Procurement at an operational level

Operation level focuses on day-to-day operations. Although procurement is rarely done for single operations, much work related to procurement can be seen as operational [22]. It can include micromanagement of works or services, working with reports, or change minor procurement documentation such as report formats for the next procurement process.

2.3 Challenges in procurement

The procurement process is not limited only to the procurement stage [23], especially dealing with procurement at strategic and tactical levels. Procurement procedure influences the execution of works, increase dynamics in the market, and eventually, they are changing ground for next procurement processes. This indicates that procurement is a complex system [5, 24]. Looking on project procurement as a complex system allows identifying some issues in this type of procurement [25, 26].

2.3.1 Information asymmetry

Information asymmetry occurs when some stakeholders have more material knowledge than the other stakeholders have. Usually a procuring stakeholder has more information than is available in the documentation [27, 28]. It can include work-related data from previous or similar projects that can be beneficial for other stakeholders. It can also be some more expectations of what the final product or service should be like. On the other hand, companies can have access to more technologies, materials, methods, or systems than they are willing to reveal in their tenders, for example, due to secrecy. This behavior, although being business and competition driven, leads to nontransparent relationships and often to less profitable deals [29]. It also creates an imbalance of power in transactions that leads to a negative influence on the market's balance.

Information asymmetry at the strategic level leads to solutions that do not satisfy all the needs of the client because not all needs were properly documented. At tactical level, information asymmetry can challenge performance due to the lack of bigger vision from companies. At an operational level, it can create problems with right executions of all regulations and reporting systems.

2.3.2 Slow and time-consuming process

The procurement procedure can affect the speed of completion. The procurement procedure itself might be very time-consuming [30]. This is especially true for procurement at the strategic level. The time between the first involvement of procurement managers in a project to the beginning of the construction work can take several years. At the early stages of the procurement process, some time is spent on preparation of specifications, the scope of work, and other terms. Usually some of the previous contracts can be reusable for these purposes; however, each set of documentation ends up being unique as it is based on individual projects. Once all is ready, request for tenders are launched with submission period of 2–8 months for more typical types of projects as for technical consultants or maintenances and even longer for building- or design-build-type contracts. After the winning contract is announced, sometime is usually reserved for negotiations and appeal. Some projects do not start immediately after but have time for companies to prepare for the start of the work. Better distributed control in the field, better connection and communication during the process of procurement, and better adaptation to the needs can make this process faster.

2.3.3 Over-specified tenders

Specifications are an important part of any tender—they help to understand what the final product or service must do. But in the same time, determining specifications is not a trivial work.

Specifications can be classified as technical and functional. Functional specifications describe what the product needs to deliver from the user's perspective. Functional specifications are in most cases considered to be more preferring. However, having only functional specifications may lead to difficulties in controlling monitoring and evaluating the product or service. Therefore, there is a need for technical specifications that describe the details and characteristics of the needed project. Technical specifications decrease openness for innovation and alternative solutions. A proper balance between technical and functional specifications is essential to avoid over-specified tenders [31]. In reality, this balance is hard to maintain because of the different goals of different stakeholders [32].

Over-specification usually is less a problem at a strategic level; but, it can be a huge issue at tactical and especially at operational levels.

2.3.4 Feedback loops

Feedback loops exist between two elements that are interconnected and that affect each other. Feedback loops are important because they show the success of project procurement compared to the outcomes [33]. For proper feedback, it would be important to analyze a set of very similar projects. However, in the case of project procurement, it cannot be done. All projects are unique, and even two similar projects may have two totally different outcomes. In addition, it takes a long time to see the outputs of the contract. Some contracts in road constructions industry can be up to 15–20 years long, thus, making the analysis of input and output variables almost impossible.

Feedbacks work in most cases well at an operational level, but at strategic and tactical levels, it is often major issues with feedback loops. At strategic levels, feedback loops hardly exist, while at tactical levels, they either nonexisting or interpretation of feedback loops happens rarely.

2.4 Traditional approaches to challenges in procurement

Several approaches exist to address some of the challenges in procurement, where each approach aims to target different scope or perspective of the issues.

2.4.1 Financial metrics

Financial metrics look on a project from the economic point of view to help to evaluate what decisions are successful and which are not. These metrics, like cost-benefit, return on investment, a total cost of ownership, can be very effective in different projects [34, 35]. However, they are more useful to determine the effectiveness of the project itself, to determine if the organization needs to own a product or it can be rented, and to determine a need to do procurement in general. Financial metrics also can be used effectively at an operational level. But they are less effective when there is a need to evaluate how good procurement is at tactical or strategic levels. Also financial metrics are not meant to include complexity that comes from communications between stakeholders because it is impossible to transform these communications into monitory values [36].

2.4.2 Simulation

A simulation uses a model to imitate real processes in the real world in a safe environment over a longer period of time. Simulation often gives a very good understanding of feedback loops, and it is a good tool to look at how the system changes over time [37]. However, a good simulation requires a good model that includes all possible interactions between stakeholders and consequences that are coming from these interactions. Although this is mostly possible, it can be extremely time-consuming, and it does not include coevolution processes in the model.

Simulation can be an effective tool for contracts for the purchase of supplies [9], where the contracts are more typical and the scope of the problem is not a holistic approach but rather figuring optimal ordering amount and reordering times. Hence, simulation of procurement at a strategic level almost never is performed because of the complexities and absent of a real system.

2.4.3 Game theory

The game theory looks at cooperation and conflicts in competitive environments. Much research in game theory field is focused on how people interact [38, 39]. Similar to simulation, game theory requires a good knowledge of all possible scenarios that can happen during the procurement. Based on this knowledge, the best solution is suggested. In the case of public project procurement, it is impossible to determine all possible scenarios and to properly define boundaries between different scenarios. It is quite common that two almost identical projects end up with one being a success, while the second fails.

In order to evaluate the success of the project procurement, the approach has to be able to see procurement holistically as a complex adaptive system.

3. Participatory simulation approach

3.1 What is a participatory simulation?

A participatory simulation, or gaming simulation, is an approach based on modeling and simulation of the real world. It uses real participants to recreate behavior and decisions in the system [40–42]. The combination allows participants to learn about the modeled system, prototype new solutions, experiment with policies, and design other changes to the system. Geurts et al. [43] states in his work that participatory simulation is a "safe environment to test strategies in advance, and can help decision-makers to create several possible futures. The players build the future conditions of the system step by step by moving from the current reality to a new vision."

A participatory simulation combines benefits of modeling and simulation with participatory methods as seen in **Figure 1** [44]. As a simulation, participatory simulation is based on a model of existing or nonexisting reality (reference system). The model is based on interdependent variables that help to formulate connections and flows in the model. It provides users with feedback on how the model changes over time. It might include decision support systems such as optimization. Also participatory simulation can be done on macro-, midi-, or microlevels. But at the same time, the participatory simulation includes "soft elements" [45]. As a method,

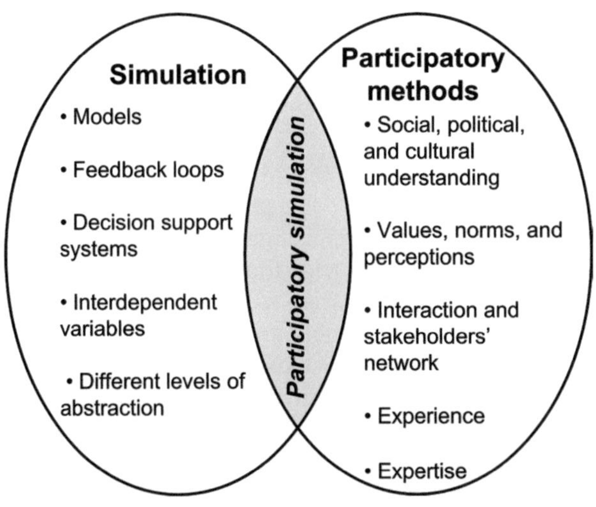

Figure 1.
Place of participatory simulation.

that involves real people, participatory simulation can handle better when the reference system deals with social, political, and/or cultural aspects. Participatory simulation allows working with value systems of participants and their perceptions. It also makes possible to investigate interaction patterns between participants. As a participatory method, it allows also to bring experience and expertise of people into the model.

3.2 Steps of participatory simulation

Although the development steps of the participatory simulation are different based on different objectives that are considered, the main elements are seen in **Figure 2**.

The participatory simulation starts with an identification of goal(s) and building proper **design** of the simulation. **Roles** indicate different types of players with their functions. **Rules** regulate what actions are allowed or forbidden. **Objectives** specify purpose and goals for participants during the simulation. **Constraints** limit a range of freedoms that participants have. Additionally to participatory simulation design, each session is affected by state and context. **State** refers to design variables, such as a number of teams or size of start budget. The **context** is related to other variables that may be relevant to the session, for example, background information of participants.

Participants are engaged in each session. Often participants are expected to have some knowledge about the system or the problem. As a result of the sessions, these participants gain some experience by participating in the simulation and by discussing the model after the session. At the same time, game produces qualitative and quantitative data, such as decisions that participants made, time that it took to make these decisions, statistic how participant performed in comparison with other participants, comments that participants made, level of stress, etc.

3.3 A participatory simulation approach for procurement

In the case of participatory simulation of procurement, the approach design is largely depended on the planning level: operational, tactical, or strategic. Each type of planning will have a different degree of realism or abstraction, and a solution will range from specific changes to a general direction where change should go (**Table 1**).

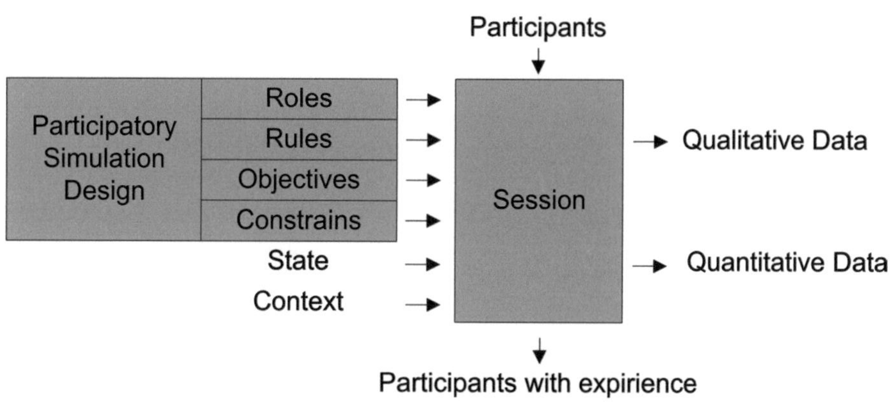

Figure 2.
Inputs and outputs of a participatory simulation session, based on [41].

Types of planning	Scope
Operational	Document scope
Tactical	Project scope
Strategic	Holistic scope (e.g., LCA scope)

Table 1.
Different scopes for project procurement participatory simulation based on different types of planning.

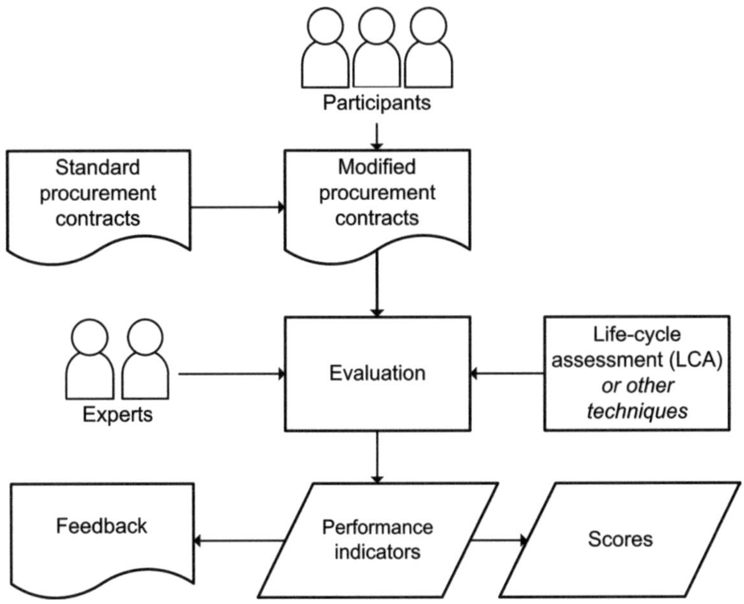

Figure 3.
Participatory simulation design.

On operational level, the focus is on an individual document or a small set of documents. It can be a specification document or description of the bonus system for performed work or any other document that affects the outcome. Participatory simulation, in this case, can help to determine how changes affect the final outputs.

Participatory simulation on a tactical level allows experimenting with the entire project. Such a project can be procured for technical consultants or procuring road maintenance. The outcome of such type of participatory simulation can be a better understanding of strength and weaknesses of business models for such types of projects; it can identify bottlenecks and documents or set of documents that need deeper evaluation.

Also participatory simulation allows looking beyond the individual type of projects on a strategic level. This gives an opportunity to analyze a set of projects in a more holistic way. For example, at this level, we can look at a combination of rural and urban projects or from road design project to road maintenance. Results from the approach at this level give an overlook on current practices in general and help to see how well different projects actually cooperate one with another.

Participatory simulation design depends on a type of planning, but generally can be as seen in **Figure 3**. The type determines what documents should be included in the design and what is the main objective.

Roles for these experiments mainly should reflect important stakeholders—transport administration employees, technical consultants, researchers, construction companies, material suppliers, etc. Roles also can include specialization such as project leaders or procurement managers. Roles are determined by potential choices that can be done in during the session.

Rules describe what documentation can be changed and what type of communication is allowed. In a case when a session has several rounds, rules can describe if the rounds are inner dependent (participant continue to round 2 on the results from round 1) or rounds are independent from one another.

Objectives specify purpose that participants have to strive to achieve in the session. It can be typical objectives based on a type of planning, such as to build a road within a limited budget. In this case, a participant or a team of participants with the lowest budget and sufficient quality can be considered the winners.

Constrains limit what participants are allowed to change and what must be kept. Often on an operational level, final solutions have to more concrete, and they must include many legal and management aspects. So participants have constrained on what has to be included in their final results. On the other hand, the strategic level solution can be almost without any constraints to give a chance for participants to be fully creative and innovative.

State and context are often defined closer to the experiment day, and they influence variables around the game. Such aspects can be the employment of participants and their role in the game. The **state** describes aspects as a number of teams, number of participants in the team, and what is the balance in scoring between the main objective and creativity. **Context** is dealing more with variables regarding participants themselves and the venue. Are we inviting to play only transport administration employees or someone from business too? Do transport administration employees have roles as transport administration employees or as a business (role reverse)? If someone from the business is invited what is his or her incentive during this experiment? Was session too short/long and participants felt pressure because of that? All of these variables affect the sessions' results but also give richness to the gained experience. Typically, sessions are repeatable with the same participatory simulation design, but state and context are always different.

4. Case studies

To show the application of a participatory simulation approach for project procurement, two case studies are selected. Both cases are related to road project procurement. However, the first case is about road construction from a life cycle perspective, while the second case is focused only on road maintenance procurement and is focused more on the details of a contract. These cases were chosen to show how the approach can be applied for a different level of planning and what outcomes can be expected.

4.1 Redesigning procurement contracts for the entire life cycle

4.1.1 Overview

Most of the work in road construction in Sweden is procured by Swedish Transport Administration (STA). Although there are multiple types of procurement contracts that they do on daily bases, one of big challenge they have is related to the procurement of technical design of roads, procurement of road construction, and procurement of road maintenance. STA occasionally tries procuring all these steps as one big project, but such results are not always successful due to high risks.

However, the current state also has issues, because final products end up with too high life cycle costs.

The purpose of the participatory simulation was to address some of the issue related to the need for redesigning procurement contracts with a strong focus on the life cycle. There was a need for an environment, where Swedish Transport Administration can think and discuss incentives in the procurement process that they offer to a business to improve the situation, as well as discuss dilemmas why some attempts to solve this resulted successfully, while other attempts were less effective than traditional approaches.

4.1.2 Participatory simulation design

To successfully reach objectives for this type of problem, it requires going beyond typical procurement contracts. Thus, a strategic level was selected for this case. At this level, it is important to let participants be more creative and focus on the bigger picture rather than small individual details. The main focus of this session was to build the best road within a limited budget. This would include typical procurement of two technical consultants, procurement of road construction, and procurement of two rounds of road maintenance. Participants could choose design-build contracts, build-maintain contracts, design-build-maintain contracts, and individual contracts, dividing into lots or any other strategy to make sure that costs for the life cycle of a road are the lowest. The expert-based model supported evaluation of the decisions and produced outcomes. To achieve it, the model was developed as seen in **Figure 4**.

It was only one **role** for participants—Transport Administration. Participants needed to use all their experience and knowledge to act in the best interests of the company. They needed to make all decisions regarding the contracts themselves, meaning that in some moments they had to act as project leaders, in other moments as procurement managers, and in some moments as a board of directors.

Rules for this case were straightforward—participants were allowed to make any changes in procurement strategies and documents that they wanted to achieve the goal. They had access to real developed and still developing business models of Swedish Transport Administration. They were given premade standard procurement documentation based on internal documentation and already published calls of tenders as found at Tender Electronic Daily (TED), an online official journal of the EU, dedicated to European public procurement. Some other rules specified that participants were not allowed to communicate with their competitors during the session.

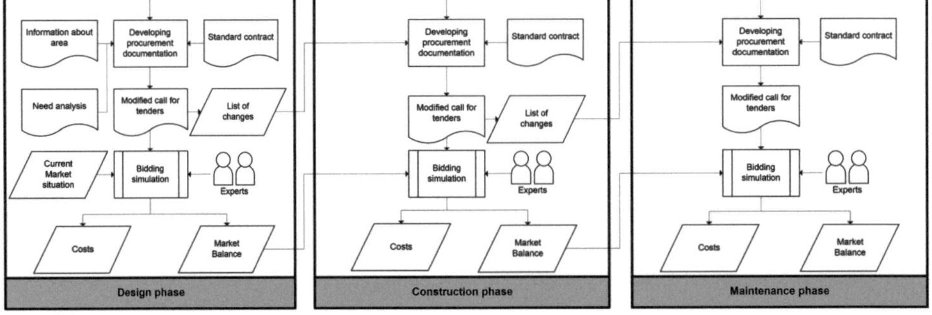

Figure 4.
Participatory simulation design for the case of redesigning procurement contracts for the entire life cycle.

They had access to "a market" (represented by an expert in the field) to procure services and works. In this case, participants had to work based on information gained from the market.

The **objective** of the simulation was to build the best road for the price with a limited budget. A lifetime of the road was given as 15 years, which is a reasonable length of the road before it requires major fixing. A definition of "the best road" intentionally was not given since it was another question about what characteristics road should have to be considered of good quality. Based on the objective, scoring system was developed as well. The scoring system provides a feedback system and helps participants to be more involved in the process. Mainly, the scoring was based on the total price of the entire road life cycle; however, some extra points were given if participants were able to address innovation, as it is one of the big priorities for the organization.

Constraints were minimal. Participants were not limited in what they can change and type of changes it could be. The only constraints were of ethical issues—participants had to be honest in their dealings.

Several **states** were defined in the session. First of all, the participants played in teams. There were four teams where each team had 2–3 participants. The session took 1 day that included 6 hours of participation time, discussion after, and few breaks during the day.

Nine **participants** were selected for this simulation (five men and four women). They are employees of procurement and strategic departments of Swedish Transport Administration, who worked in the road construction field from 18 to 34 years and have good knowledge of project management, procurement processes, and Swedish Transport Administration's strategic goals. Teams were organized naturally based on who preferred to work with whom.

4.1.3 Results

Two teams (team A and team B) produced full design-build-maintain projects where all design, consulting, and construction on maintenance responsibilities are part of procured work and services. Still, team A decided to focus more on increasing innovation in processes and materials; team B worked on increasing interest in the market for the project. Both teams have decrease number of technical specifications and remove many documents from the standard set that is used for a request for tenders to increase transparency.

The third team, team C, decided to develop a design of road using in-house experts rather than procure it and then combine building and maintenance together. In their building-maintenance documentation, they tried to have more functional specifications.

Team D procured each work process individually. However, they decided not to follow the approved by the organization guidelines but instead used their experiences as working as entrepreneurs to focus only on important elements (**Table 2**).

All changes were done by editing standard contract templates. Most of the changes included removing parts of contracts as seen in **Figure 5**, or even removing some documents completely, and also by adding some guidelines on what needs to be expanded.

The total costs without any changes were calculated as 110 million dollars. However, teams had a game budget of 80 million to stimulate creative thinking. Team A had the lowest results with total costs of 71 million, team B was second with 75 million, and team D was with 78 million. Team C went over the budget with 88 million dollars, but even this was way under the original costs.

In the discussion after the exercise, participants indicated that success for this type of projects required more collaboration with business partners. One participant said: "We focus on the life cycle cost to find the lowest possible LCC. Then we

	Team A	Team B	Team C	Team D
Number of participants	2	2	2	3
Average work experience in the field	26 years	24.5 years	29 years	27.3 years
Proposed solution cost	71 million dollars	75 million dollars	88 million dollars	78 million dollars
Solution cost comparison to base cost*	Improved by 35.5%	Improved by 31.8%	Improved by 20%	Improved by 29.1%
Main strategy	Design-build-maintain project	Design-build-maintain project	Each work process procured individually	Design by in-house experts and build-maintain project
Final score**	89 points	86 points	81 points	85 points

**A base cost for a project with no changes is 110 million dollars.*
***A final score for a project with no changes is 50 points. The teams aimed to maximize their final score.*

Table 2.
Information and results from the redesigning procurement contracts for the entire life cycle.

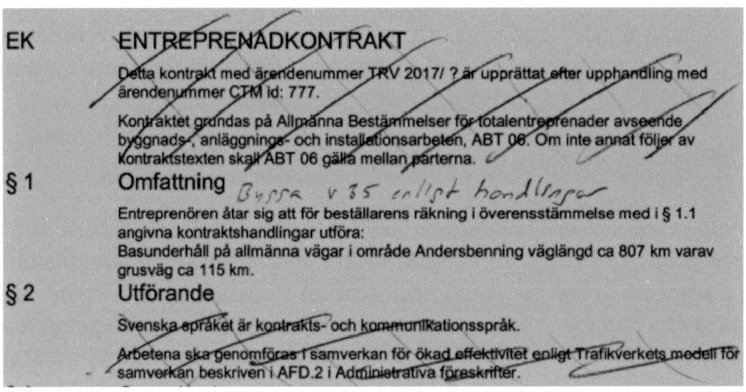
EK ENTREPRENADKONTRAKT

Detta kontrakt med ärendenummer TRV 2017/ ? är upprättat efter upphandling med ärendenummer CTM id: 777.

Kontraktet grundas på Allmänna Bestämmelser för totalentreprenader avseende byggnads-, anläggnings- och installationsarbeten, ABT 06. Om inte annat följer av kontraktstexten skall ABT 06 gälla mellan parterna.

§ 1 Omfattning

Entreprenören åtar sig att för beställarens räkning i överensstämmelse med i § 1.1 angivna kontraktshandlingar utföra:
Basunderhåll på allmänna vägar i område Andersbenning väglängd ca 807 km varav grusväg ca 115 km.

§ 2 Utförande

Svenska språket är kontrakts- och kommunikationsspråk.

Arbetena ska genomföras i samverkan för ökad effektivitet enligt Trafikverkets modell för samverkan beskriven i AFD.2 i Administrativa föreskrifter.

Figure 5.
Example of some changes by team A in documents describing some administrative information.

thought that we want to invite suppliers for early involvement, to write the specifications and to make the whole contract as good as possible. And we would like to bring suppliers early because they have huge knowledge." Also they emphasized that there is need to be more open to the plans and information.

At the same time, some of the current issues where identified. One of the biggest issues was how to deal with over-specified tenders. One participant mentioned: "Sometimes it is a fact that we standardize too much, and does it really matter if the noise barriers are different in the north than in the south of Sweden? No, it does not matter. What matters if they are working or not?" Some other issues were identified as a lack of information about some important aspects, for example, how successful were the completed projects, while for some other aspects are too much information and regulations. As one participant mentioned: "One of the issues is that we have all these business models. We are talking about them all the time everywhere. But in reality, we just speak about the same complexity and uncertainty, just presented in different ways. And as a result, we have three or more different solutions for exactly the same problem."

In general, participants had a positive experience with some advice and suggestions on how to address this type of contracts. One participant said: "I also think that it was good to think outside the box. We don't dare to think like this, because we hear every day: 'you cannot do that, you cannot do that, you cannot do that.' Nevertheless, we tried to do it now freely!"

4.2 Improving existing procurement for road maintenance

4.2.1 Overview

Maintenance contracts are seen as a type of contracts with the lowest amount of innovation and that raises many concerns of the Swedish Transport Administration. Maintenance contracts are highly standardized across entire Sweden, and they contain a large number of technical specifications and regulations on how maintenance has to be carried out. An average number of bidders is around two to five offers per request for tenders.

The main objective of a participatory simulation was to determine what elements need to be changed to make maintenance contracts more attractive for the contractors. The problem here was that contracts cannot change too much due to high requirements for the quality, but they cannot stay the same because a number of bidders are too low.

4.2.2 Participatory simulation design

The design for such a simulation needed to include the entire scope of the project to identify where bottlenecks are in the system. Hence, the tactical level was chosen for the design. Since maintenance contracts are extremely standardized, it was chosen to build an entire experiment on one of the existing maintenance contracts. A combination of expert-based model and an analytical model was used in this simulation as seen in **Figure 6.**

All participants again had only one **role**—Transport Administration. The **objective** was to develop three cycles of project procurement (each cycle takes 4–6 years in real life). Participants needed to reduce their costs by at least 20% comparing to real prices. Scoring was done mainly based on price, but a set of other parameters (quality, environment, innovation, number of bidders, etc.) was used as smaller friction for scoring.

The **rules** were that contracts have to feel real, meaning that participants needed to produce procurement documentation that can be published even in a real situation. Quality of roads and market situation were inner connected between rounds.

Participants had some **constraints** on time (each round lasted 2 hours and they had to publish a request for tender in the end), on documentation (all important documents had to be included), and on a budget (prices could not go more than 20% comparing to real prices).

The session was split into five 2-hour-long meetings, where the first meeting was an introduction and the last one was a discussion. Three meetings in between were three session rounds. Eight participants were selected (three men and five women), who played in teams of two with totally four teams. All participants were employees of Swedish Transport Administration, who work together in maintenance procurement department in one of the regional offices.

4.2.3 Results

Most of the teams decided to go with minimum changes, mainly editing some structures of the files to make them more readable. Some suggested adding extra

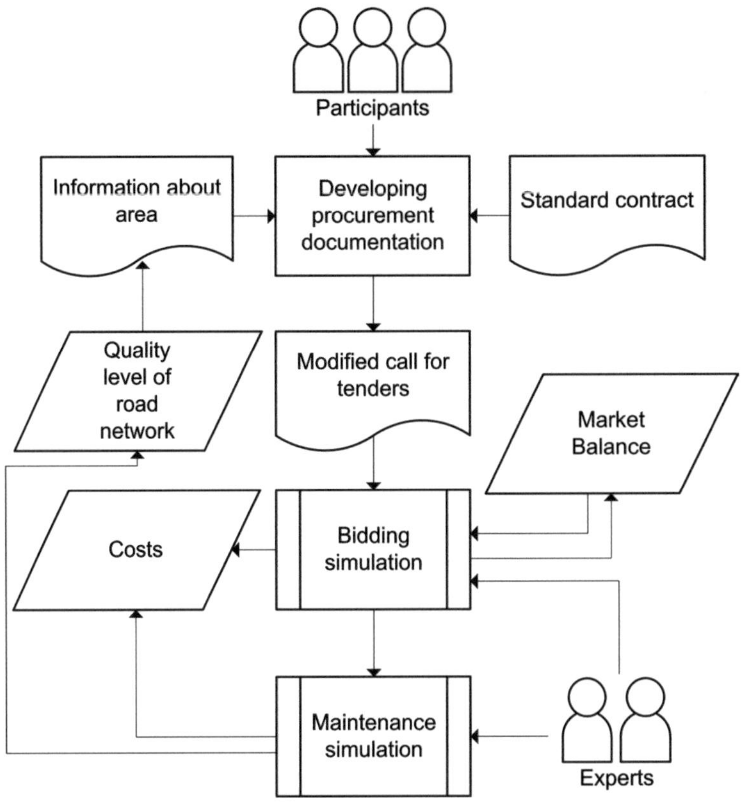

Figure 6.
Participatory simulation design for the case of improving existing procurement for road maintenance.

incentives, such as bonus system for good performance. One team tried to invest more money during the first cycle to improve the quality of the road network, and then spend less to just maintain achieved high quality (**Table 3**).

Majority of participants commented about needs for STA to be more open with its preferences. One person said they need to "get away from the speculative prices on certain works that leads to over or under-production because of how the contractors calculate prices." Other person mentioned: "we must make the structure of the contracts easier to understand both for Swedish Transport Administration and for contractors."

Some other comments indicated that this issue will have certain costs, especially in the beginning. One participant commented: "A focus on the increase of the contractors to make innovation possible by increasing costs." Another comment about team strategy was: "We took away a lot of documents and we open up and made a lot of risks on STA, but it was needed to be done."

An issue of standardization was discussed in this case study as well. As one participant said: "We've standardized contracts for many years and done it very well and got a really good national governance, but now, maybe, we have to move on and open up a bit to get that difference into the contracts based on conditions at the geography."

Participants also were keen on using participatory simulation approach. One of the participants commented on experience after the session: "I think there are a lot of ideas at a regional or a local level. To evaluate them in terms of the success one can ask 'What's the worst that can happen?'"

	Team A	Team B	Team C	Team D
Number of participants	2	2	2	2
Average work experience in the field	11.5 years	7.5 years	13 years	16.5 years
Proposed solution cost	33.2	35.6	35	30.3
Solution cost comparison to base cost*	Worsen by 3.8%	Worsen by 11.3%	Worsen by 9.4%	Improved by 5.3%
Main strategy	Reduce the risk of the contractor and increase degrees of freedom	Provide more incentives for innovation	Push for innovation, support new technology, and improve customer dialog	Restructure entire contract, provide better economic incentives
Final score**	116 points	101 points	113 points	123 points

**A base cost for a project with no changes is 32 million dollars.*
***A final score for a project with no changes is 80 points. The teams aimed to maximize their final score.*

Table 3.
Information and results from the case of improving existing procurement for road maintenance.

4.3 Summary of case studies

Two case studies were selected to demonstrate how a participatory simulation approach can address issues with project procurement. It was observed that participatory simulation helped in:

- Achieving assigned objectives of each case
- Experiencing effects of information asymmetry
- Facing results of the fast-paced procurement cycle
- Addressing issues of over-specification
- Making an analysis of feedback loops
- Working in an open environment without punishment for risk-taking

An objective for each case was achieved. Participatory simulation created an environment in with participants could discuss safety problems and concerns and experiment with different solutions. This approach helped in allocating some bottlenecks and providing scenarios for how they can be resolved in real life. Even more, the models could be easily adapted for other objectives as well.

The participatory simulation also helped in explaining the reasons and dangers of information asymmetry. Some benefits of open information were defined, and sources of the issue were discussed.

Another benefit of this approach comes from the fast pace of simulation. Performing the entire procurement cycle from the need of definition to tender award in only a few hours instead of several months helped to have a unique perspective on the procurement process. It helped to find some issues and to think more outside the scope of just an individual project.

Problems of over-specification were raised up both during simulation sessions and after in discussions. Participants acknowledged issues that came from too many specifications and standardization policies.

An opportunity to have more feedback then just a final price helped to focus on some aspects of a procurement process that typically are ignored.

In general, it was observed that the open environment during participatory simulation without punishment for risk-taking allowed more creative and constructive solutions and discussion. Similar outcomes are hard to achieve in the real world due to the nature of the work.

5. Conclusions

Project procurement is common in fields where systems are large-scale and complex, and they require good planning before any changes can be implemented. These complexities often lead to a situation in which the procurement process, especially when part of a project, can rarely match the objectives of organizations. It is often related to information asymmetry in the sector, slow procuring process, over-specified tenders, and poor feedbacks. Traditional methods that are used in this field can help to some extent, but they cannot address all issues since they do not evaluate project procurement holistically.

An effective approach to look at the whole system proved to be participatory simulation. Two cases are described in order to explore how this participatory simulation approach can help to investigate different issues that exist in road project procurements.

The first case was focused on redesigning procurement contracts for the entire road life cycle. Participants needed to develop procurement contracts for a road from cradle to grave, including procurement of consultants for design, procurement of construction works, and procurement of maintenance. Participants had full freedom to make any changes they wish.

The second case was about improving current contracts for road maintenance. Participants needed to modify a standard procurement contact with the aim of a long-term increase in innovation. Participants had to use current work procedures, but they were free to change documentation that was attached.

In both cases, participatory simulation helped to determine the bottlenecks of the system and produced outcomes that could be used to develop guidelines for further changes in the real system. It also allowed experimenting with different policies and business models to see what solutions are more suitable for different situations. Based on case studies, we can conclude that the effects of different strategies and policies in project procurement can be observed and researched using participatory simulation.

Participatory simulation allows for investigating procurement processes on different levels of planning to search for bottlenecks and underlying issues. This approach also deals well with common challenges in procurement, providing an environment where participants can experiment and gain feedback within a short period of time. Based on these findings, this approach can be used to study the institutional, governance, social, and contractual setting of project procurement. The challenges and issues discussed in this work are not specific only to the road construction sector, and the proposed solution can be used in other fields as well that deal with the complexity of the procurement process.

Author details

Maksims Kornevs*, Jannicke Baalsrud Hauge and Sebastiaan Meijer
KTH Royal Institute of Technology, Stockholm, Sweden

*Address all correspondence to: kornevs@kth.se

References

[1] OECD. Size of Public Procurement. Government at a Glance 2017. Paris: OECD Publishing; 2017. pp. 172-173

[2] European Parliament and of the Council. Directive 2014/24/EU of the European Parliament and of the Council of 26 February 2014 on Public Procurement and Repealing Directive 2004/18/EC. 2014

[3] Thai KV. Public procurement re-examined. Journal of Public Procurement. 2001;**1**(1):9-50

[4] Croom SR, Brandon-Jones A. Key issues in e-procurement: Procurement implementation and operation in the public sector. Journal of Public Procurement. 2005;**5**(3):367-387

[5] Kornevs M, Kringos N, Meijer S. Perspectives of stakeholders on road procurements: In search of procurement aspects using Q methodology. In: CESUN 2016 Conference. 2016. pp. 1-8

[6] Eriksson M. Procurement of complex technical systems: Strategies for successful projects [thesis]. Stockholm: KTH Royal Institute of Technology. 2005. Available from: http://urn.kb.se/resolve?urn=urn:nbn:se:kth:diva-593

[7] Altamirano MA. Innovative Contracting Practices in the Road Sector: Cross-National Lessons in Dealing with Opportunistic Behaviour. Delft: Next Generation Infrastructures Foundation; 2010

[8] Crespo Marquez A, Blanchar C. The procurement of strategic parts. Analysis of a portfolio of contracts with suppliers using a system dynamics simulation model. International Journal of Production Economics. 2004;**88**(1):29-49

[9] Keay L, Keenan CA, Ricketts JA, Schaefer WS. Simulation of Business Transformation Outsourcing of Sourcing, Procurement and Payables [Internet]. 2003. Available from: https://patents.google.com/patent/US7548872B2/en [cited: 08 February 2018]

[10] Baily P, Farmer D, Crocker B, Jessop D, Jones D. Procurement Principles and Management. 10th ed. New York: Prentice Hall Financial Times; 2008. 468 p

[11] United Nations. Procurement Practitioner's Handbook. Denmark: United Nations High Level Committee on Management, Procurement Network; 2017. p. 209

[12] de Araújo MCB, Alencar LH, de Miranda Mota CM. Project procurement management: A structured literature review. International Journal of Project Management. 2017;**35**(3):353-377

[13] Holt GD. Classifying construction contractors. Building Research and Information. 1997;**25**(6):374-382

[14] Rowlinson S, McDermott P. Procurement Systems: A Guide to Best Practice in Construction. Abingdon: Routledge; 2005. 317 p

[15] Svenson K. Estimated lifetimes of road pavements in Sweden using time-to-event analysis. Journal of Transportation Engineering. 2014;**140**(11):04014056

[16] Van Belle J-F, Temmerman M, Schenkel Y. Three level procurement of forest residues for power plant. Biomass and Bioenergy. 2003;**24**(4):401-409

[17] Spekman RE. A strategic approach to procurement planning. Journal of Purchasing & Supply Management. 1981;**17**(4):2-8

[18] Bratt C, Hallstedt S, Robèrt K-H, Broman G, Oldmark J. Assessment

of criteria development for public procurement from a strategic sustainability perspective. Journal of Cleaner Production. 2013;**52**:309-316

[19] Bovaird T. Developing new forms of partnership with the 'market' in the procurement of public services. Public Administration. 2006;**84**(1):81-102

[20] Beaudoin D, Frayret J-M, LeBel L. Hierarchical forest management with anticipation: An application to tactical–operational planning integration. Canadian Journal of Forest Research. 2008;**38**(8):2198-2211

[21] van de Velde D, Pruijmboom E. First Experiences with Tendering at the Tactical Level (Service Design) in Dutch Public Transport. In: 8th Conference on Competition and Ownership in Land Passenger Transport. Rio de Janeiro, Brazil; 2003

[22] Telgen J, Harland C, Knight L, Harland C, Knight L. Public procurement in perspective. In: Public Procurement International Cases and Commentary. Abingdon: Routledge; 2012. Available from: https://www.taylorfrancis.com/ [cited: 21 May 2019]

[23] Callender G, Matthews D. The economic context of government procurement: New challenges and new opportunities. Journal of Public Procurement. 2002;**2**(2):216-236

[24] Holland JH. Complex adaptive systems. Daedalus. 1992;**121**(1):17-30

[25] Uyarra E, Edler J, Garcia-Estevez J, Georghiou L, Yeow J. Barriers to innovation through public procurement: A supplier perspective. Technovation. 2014;**34**(10):631-645

[26] Erridge A, Nondi R. Public procurement, competition and partnership. European Journal of Purchasing & Supply Management. 1994;**1**(3):169-179

[27] Corbett CJ, Tang CS. Designing supply contracts: Contract type and information asymmetry. In: Quantitative Models for Supply Chain Management. Boston, MA: Springer; 1999. pp. 269-297. Available from: https://link.springer.com/chapter/10.1007/978-1-4615-4949-9_9

[28] Mukhopadhyay SK, Yue X, Zhu X. A Stackelberg model of pricing of complementary goods under information asymmetry. International Journal of Production Economics. 2011;**134**(2):424-433

[29] Gümüş M, Ray S, Gurnani H. Supply-side story: Risks, guarantees, competition, and information asymmetry. Management Science. 2012;**58**(9):1694-1714

[30] Matthews J, Love PED, Heinemann S, Chandler R, Rumsey C, Olatunj O. Real time progress management: Re-engineering processes for cloud-based BIM in construction. Automation in Construction. 2015;**58**:38-47

[31] Vähätalo M, Kallio TJ. Public procurement for innovations: Barriers in health and social services. In: IRSPM. 2017. Available from: http://urn.kb.se/resolve?urn=urn:nbn:se:lnu:diva-68764

[32] Iossa E, Waterson M. Maintaining competition in recurrent procurement contracts: A case study on the London bus market. Transport Policy;**75**:141-149. Available from: http://www.sciencedirect.com/science/article/pii/S0967070X16300762

[33] Kornevs M, Kringos N, Meijer S. Developing a system dynamics model from perceptions. In: 32nd Annual Q Conference. 2016. p. 1-9

[34] Kornevs M, Minkevica V, Holm M. Cloud computing evaluation based on financial metrics. Information Technology and Management Science. 2012;**15**(1):87-92

[35] Nolte M. The Impact of Sales and Operations Planning Implementation on Supply Chain and Financial Metrics. Knoxville: University of Tennessee; 2015

[36] Meehan J, Menzies L, Michaelides R. The long shadow of public policy: Barriers to a value-based approach in healthcare procurement. Journal of Purchasing and Supply Management. 2017;**23**(4):229-241

[37] Robinson S. Simulation: The Practice of Model Developmentand Use. 1st ed. Chichester, West Sussex, England; Hoboken, NJ: John Wiley & Sons; 2003

[38] Chen ET. The gamification as a resourceful tool to improve work performance. In: Reiners T, Wood LC, editors. Gamification in Education and Business. Berlin: Springer International Publishing; 2015. pp. 473-488. Available from: http://link.springer.com/chapter/10.1007/978-3-319-10208-5_24

[39] Morrow JD. Game Theory for Political Scientists. Princeton, NJ: Princeton University Press; 1994. 376 p

[40] Duke RD, Geurts J. Policy Games for Strategic Management. Amsterdam: Rozenberg Publishers; 2004. 376 p

[41] Grogan P, Meijer S. Gaming methods in engineering systems research. Systems Engineering. 2017;**20**(6):542-552

[42] Meijer S. The Organisation of Transactions: Studying Supply Networks Using Gaming Simulation. Wageningen: Wageningen Publishers; 2009

[43] Geurts JLA, Duke RD, Vermeulen PAM. Policy gaming for strategy and change. Long Range Planning. 2007;**40**(6):535-558

[44] Kornevs M. Assessment of application of participatory methods for complex adaptive systems in the public sector [thesis]. Stockholm: KTH Royal Institute of Technology; 2019

[45] Ernst A, Biß KH, Shamon H, Schumann D, Heinrichs HU. Benefits and challenges of participatory methods in qualitative energy scenario development. Technological Forecasting and Social Change. 2018;**127**:245-257

Chapter 4

Software Design Considerations for Mathematics in Mobile Games

Katherine Smith, Yuzhong Shen and Anthony Dean

Abstract

A software system has been designed and developed to allow for the display, symbolic manipulation, and player entry of mathematics expressions in mobile games. Display, manipulation, and entry of mathematical expressions are traditionally difficult tasks. Increased limitations on screen space and user input when developing for mobile devices only exacerbate these difficulties. The developed software system balances considerations for ease of use and user interaction with the desire for players to be able to enter answers in a way that is more flexible and interactive than multiple choice, which is the dominant method of interactions in serious games. The software system uses a modular design to separate symbolic math software components from math display components to facilitate reuse of the software system. Additionally, the system displays mathematical expression in a way that is consistent with textbook and handwritten notations to ease the transition between the game and the classroom. Finally, the system provides affordances for natural user interaction to promote usability and engagement. This system has been used to develop a mobile game designed to help students master introductory calculus and physics at the undergraduate level.

Keywords: game design, serious games, user interaction, STEM education, human factors

1. Introduction

There are many interventions in higher education that can be implemented through mobile games. Presenting these interventions using mobile applications is supported by the fact that 92% of higher education students own at least two mobile devices [1]. Further, characteristics of mobile technology are converging with well-known pedagogical principles as they simultaneously evolve to become more personalized, learner centered, and ubiquitous [2]. Research into mobile learning effectiveness shows positive results. Additionally, incorporating mobile devices into mathematics courses specifically leads to enhanced student perception of learning mathematics [3], which has been shown to be a stronger indicator of positive outcomes than previous academic success [4].

Traditionally, individuals needed to learn systems with unique languages, such as LaTeX or MathML, in order to produce readable mathematical content electronically. Further, text input on mobile devices is difficult and cumbersome [5] and students identify hindrances typing or entering answers on mobile devices [6]. For mobile games in mathematics and most other STEM courses, it is necessary to display and manipulate mathematical expressions and formulas. In mathematics, even entering a simple expression can require many more screen taps than one would expect which can lead to student frustration [7]. This is an issue that must be overcome as student perception of the ease of use and usefulness of mobile learning is correlated with the likelihood that they will use it in their coursework [8]. Particularly in mathematics, difficulties include display, manipulation and user input of mathematical expressions and use of symbolic methods to determine whether or not an answer is correct [9]. Complicating this further is the difficulty of balancing the limited interface with small screen size in order to provide a positive user experience [10].

Finally, there have been many concerns raised by educators and instructional designers that indicate the importance of focusing on curricular goals as the primary focus during the development of applications for mathematics education [11, 12]. Focusing on the curriculum means not only teaching the right content but teaching and displaying the content in the right way so that the knowledge students obtain from a mobile application translates into the classroom. One way this can be facilitated is by using a system that allows for the correct display, manipulation, and input of mathematical expressions and objects. While there are many computer-aided algebra systems available, many of these are either proprietary or require some method of coding the input to get the desired result making them difficult to embed in mobile applications or difficult for students to use [13].

To embed mathematics directly into mobile games, the authors have created a modular system that focuses on allowing students to easily, but freely, input expressions that are comparable with expressions in their textbooks while keeping the number of screen taps low. This software system incorporates simplicity and interactivity which have been identified as key contributors to overall usability in user interface design [10]. In addition, the system is implemented in two modules. The first is a set of classes that allow for symbolic manipulation. The second is a set of classes that aid in the manipulation and display of the expressions inside a game engine. By incorporating these classes in a game engine, other mobile applications developed in the same game engine can incorporate the work relatively easily. By keeping the symbolic classes separate, the system can be ported to a different game engine by only modifying the display classes.

The remainder of this chapter is organized as follows: Section 2 explores related work, Section 3 details the methods used to develop the system, Section 4 provides results from implementing the system in an educational STEM game, and Section 5 concludes the chapter and discusses recommendations for future work.

2. Related work

There are several examples of mobile applications that help students practice mathematical concepts up to calculus. While most of these are not games, reviewing them shows what has been accomplished in mobile mathematics display.

One example of a mobile application with practice problems in math including topics up to differential equations and multivariable calculus is Khan Academy [14]. Khan Academy is a free repository for content but has been adding questions to their website and mobile application. Another example is IXL Math [15]. This application, which requires a paid subscription, includes practice problems up to calculus. Additionally, there are numerous examples of mathematics in games for content at and below the level of basic algebra.

The previously mentioned applications tend to limit the keyboard input by problem type. If a problem does not require trigonometric functions, then these input keys will not be available. Recently, Nakamura and Nakahara developed an interface for mathematics input that limits the number of screen taps [7]. They accomplished this by opening a submenu when a key is touched. The user then flicks up, down, left or right to insert the corresponding symbol.

The only game to the best of our knowledge that incorporates math beyond algebra is a game previously developed by the authors to cover topics in precalculus [13]. This game employed external Python libraries to generate images of the expressions needed in the game. When this communication was done at run time, there was a noticeable delay between the function call and display of the expression. Additionally, interaction was limited because the expressions were generated as images and it is almost impossible to detect user interactions with mathematical symbols embedded in images. Finally, it was necessary to distribute the core components of a Python installation with the game which increased the package size, making mobile deployment infeasible. Generating the images in advance eliminated the delay and decreased the package size but removed the ability to randomly generate problems in real time.

3. Methods

The purpose for developing this software system is to create a solution that allows for display, symbolic computation, and answer entry for introductory, undergraduate STEM courses including first courses in calculus and physics. Typical introductory calculus problems include derivatives and integrals of various functions such as polynomial, rational, and trigonometric functions. By knowing the most prevalent types of functions, templates were created for the terms of each function type. The template functions can be added by the player and then modified to construct a complete answer to a problem. While this system does not address every problem type in undergraduate STEM courses, the methodology provides a flexible model that can handle a range of common problems. Additionally, the model can be extended by developers to cover additional problem types as needed.

The modular system developed has the following characteristics:

1. Using a consistent software design that supports both expression display and symbolic manipulation and comparison.

2. Controlling spacing and sizing to optimize both overall size, for readability, and relative size of expression components, for understandability.

3. Providing affordances to support natural user interaction. That is, displaying objects in the interface in a way that makes it clear how a user can interact with them.

For this system, a major goal was to provide a user experience that allowed for more variability in question answer formatting than multiple choice or matching. To accomplish this, it was necessary to develop a system that could display a problem, perform symbolic manipulations to automatically generate the correct answer, read in the user's answer, and compare it to the correct answer.

3.1 Software design for manipulation and display

Two parallel sets of classes were developed. Since the current mobile application was developed in Unity [16, 17], the classes handling the display needed to be closely linked to game objects and their properties. However, the classes handling the symbolic mathematics are only dependent on mathematics itself. Therefore, the symbolic math classes could be well separated from the display classes to facilitate reuse of the symbolic classes on different development platforms.

3.1.1 Development of symbolic math classes

Since many operations in mathematics are binary operations, mathematical expressions can be represented as a binary expression tree (**Figure 1a**). Because the operations of multiplication and addition are both associative, limiting those operations to two children was not necessary. This restriction was eliminated to make checking of expressions easier by allowing more than two terms that are added or multiplied to be stored in a list (**Figure 1b**). There are two types of nodes. Internal nodes are operations while leaf nodes are single terms. To emulate this in code, a set of three abstract classes was developed (**Figure 2**). These three classes are intentionally kept very general. Abstract classes allow methods to be defined without implementation. Every MathObject can be simplified, differentiated, and integrated, but the process for each operation varies for different types of mathematical objects and therefore must be defined in the classes derived from MathObject. Therefore, the MathObject class only provides these common functions that are applicable to expressions and their individual terms. The MathTerm class assumes that each term has a lead coefficient, exponent, and argument coefficient and that there is some convention for sorting these terms which will assist with symbolic comparison of two expressions. The expression class assumes that an expression is a list of MathObjects (either Expressions or MathTerms) that will be associated by some binary mathematical operation.

An example of a class deriving from MathTerm would be a TrigTerm. A generic trigonometric term can be written as follows:

$$a \sin^{b}(cx) \tag{1}$$

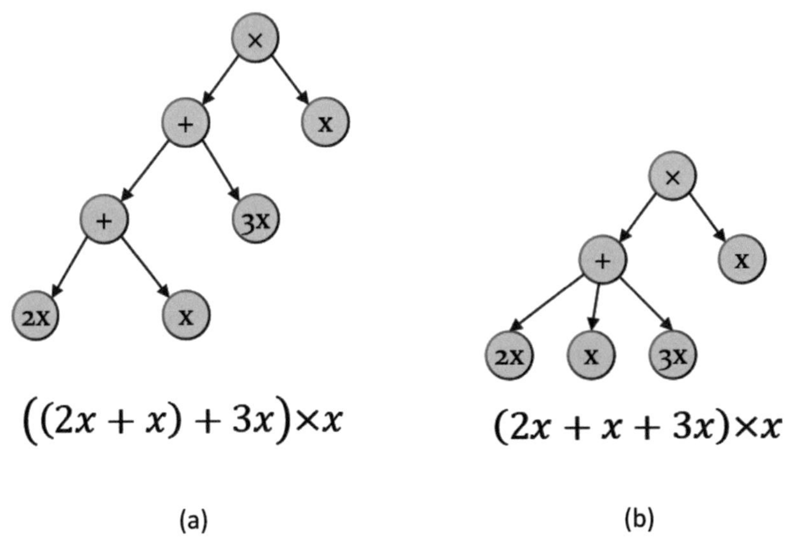

Figure 1.
(a) Traditional binary expression tree with equivalent mathematical expression. (b) Modified expression tree used in this work.

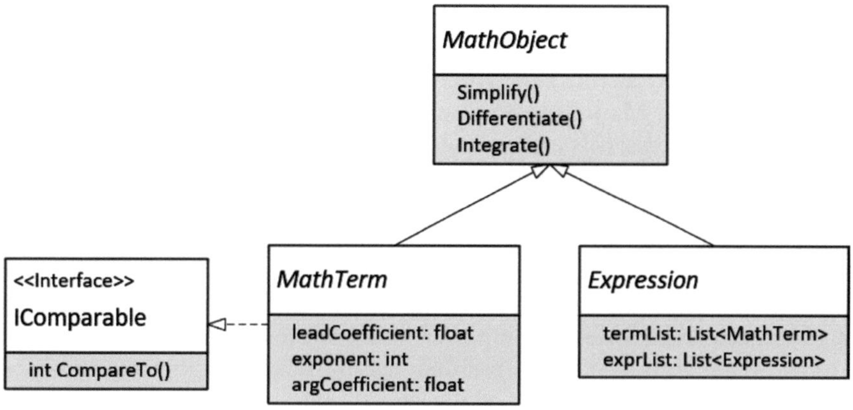

Figure 2.
Class diagram for abstract MathObject class and two derived classes, which have derived classes that are not shown in this class diagram.

In Eq. (1), a corresponds to the *leadCoefficient*, b corresponds to the exponent, and c corresponds to the *argCoefficient*. Additionally, an enumerated variable listing the allowable trigonometric functions is required.

Using just those four variables, methods to simplify, differentiate, and integrate a TrigTerm can be defined. For example, the differentiate function has a switch statement in which each case is determined by the trigonometric function type. The result of the differentiate method is an expression that is equivalent to the derivative of the term. Other examples of classes deriving from the MathTerm class are polynomial, rational, logarithmic, exponential, and so on.

An example of a class that can be derived from the expression class is a sum class. This class includes methods for simplifying sums by combining terms that are considered like terms. Polymorphism is utilized to allow use of various methods to determine which terms are like based on the type of each term. Additionally, the class includes overloaded operators that allow addition and multiplication of two sums or a sum and an individual term. This allows the developer to use more common notation to combine expressions. Since many mathematical expressions are handled through individual MathTerm objects, the only other expression class required so far has been a product class. Of course, differences and quotients can be represented using sums and products, so these are naturally included.

In addition to being able to express longer equations by combining individual terms through sums (differences) and products (quotients), the next level of complexity would be composite functions, i.e., functions formed by substituting one function into another function. While these are not handled in the current implementation, they would be an easy extension. Once the actual function substitution is handled, derivatives can be expressed as a product using the chain rule. Since the chain rule is recursive, only a few additional functions would need to be defined to achieve a complete implementation for composite functions.

3.1.2 Development of display classes

Once the issue of symbolic storage and manipulation is handled, the next step is to determine a way for the expressions to be displayed to the user in a manner that is consistent with textbook and handwritten notation. To preserve flexibility, a set of paired classes was designed for each class derived from MathTerm (**Figure 3**). This way if the code is ported to a different tool, the symbolic part can be easily reused.

The symbolic classes could be reused directly while the display classes would need to be rewritten for the target game engine.

An abstract TermController class was designed to handle the connection between the symbolic MathTerm class and the rendered game object. The TermController assumes that each term is composed of a list of component game objects that each have an assigned type, such as coefficient, variable, exponent, parenthesis, and so on. Additionally, each term is a part of a list of MathTerms and has an operator that connects it to other elements in the list as well as a button to delete the term. Finally, the TermController contains a list of modifiable components. This is a subset of the list of component game objects and indicates which components can be modified by the player. When the term is used for player input, each of the item in this list can be modified. For example, operators can be changed from plus to minus or times. Additionally, coefficient values can be changed. When the term is fixed as part of a problem statement, these objects are fixed as well and cannot be modified.

The TermController also provides virtual functions for updating the term values and controlling the spacing for display. These functions should be overridden by each subclass to handle cases for each term type. Since each TermController is associated with a MathTerm of a given type, a generic class inheriting from the TermController class is used as a bridge between the abstract term controller class and the derived classes. Generic classes have one or more type parameters. The generic class inheriting from the abstract TermController class has a single type parameter that must be a derived class of MathTerm. For clarity, we will refer to this class as TermController<T>. This type parameter is used to declare the myTerm variable which indicates the MathTerm that is associated with the TermController. This also allows for additional methods that are required for all TermController objects regardless of the type of the associated MathTerm, such as setting whether the term can be modified and deleting the term.

Like the derived classes from the MathTerm class, derived classes of the TermController<T> class specified were developed for each function type to handle unique aspects of display associated with that function type. An example of one of

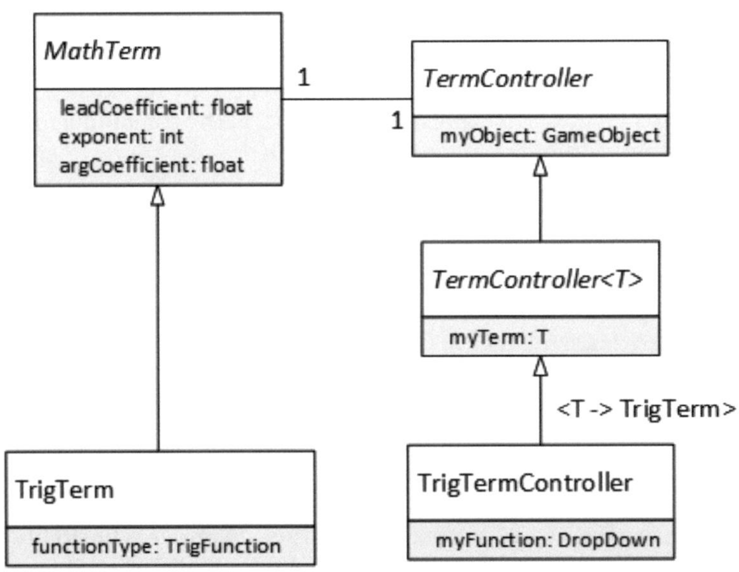

Figure 3.
Class diagram showing symbolic and display class.

these derived classes is TrigTermController which is associated with a TrigTerm by inheriting from TermController<TrigTerm>. This class has Text component variables for the lead coefficient, argument coefficient, and exponent and a DropDown component variable for the trigonometric function. These are modifiable components. Additionally, the TrigTermController class provides methods to control spacing within the term based on space available and methods for visually updating the modifiable components as well as updating the associated TrigTerm. Similar classes derived from the TermController<T> class have been developed for each class derived from MathTerm.

3.2 Adaptive sizing for display

On mobile devices, screen size is limited and therefore sizing and positioning for maximum readability without losing information is important. In mathematical expressions, this has implications at two levels. At the individual term level, the sizing and placement of parts of the expression convey meaning. The simplest examples include exponents and fractions such as y^6 and $\frac{1}{4}$, respectively. At the expression level, keeping sizing consistent for parts of terms, rather than just terms, enhances readability and understandability. For example, in an expression containing a trigonometric term with an exponent and a polynomial term, the exponents should be approximately the same size.

Methods for screen space sizing and positioning make it easy to control the sizing of terms relative to each other and the sizing of their parts relative to term size. This means that it is easy to make a trigonometric term and a polynomial term the same size overall. However, that means that their corresponding parts will not be the same size. To address this, custom methods were developed at the TermController level as well as the overall expression level to ensure consistency.

At the individual term level, it was important to establish a consistent rule for the sizing relationship between components. A static dictionary was created at the TermController level to dictate the relative widths of coefficients, variables, exponents, and so on. Another static variable was created and used to set the aspect ratio of each character. The aspect ratio allowed for the height of any character to be calculated given its width, or vice versa. These values were manipulated by the developers to come up with constant values that resulted in the display and adaptive sizing being visually consistent with a textbook presentation.

To size components adaptively based on the space available, the width of a term was calculated by summing the theoretical widths of all its components, considering that numeric terms have more than one digit. This overall term width is used to calculate a standard unit of width by dividing the maximum space the term can occupy by the overall width. Next, the height of the term is calculated by dividing the width unit by the character aspect ratio. Finally, it is determined whether the width or height is the limiting factor and the entire term is scaled accordingly by redefining the width unit if necessary. All calculations are based in screen space and it is assumed that each term can occupy a box with a given width and height. This overall box will be sized to control the ratio of the size of this term to other terms in the expression.

Once all terms are sized individually, they need to be scaled relative to other terms in the same expression. To accomplish this, the width units for the controllers are compared to find the controller that is using the smallest width. This width is then used as the standard width to resize each term based on its overall length and the available space. As a result, each term is scaled by the ratio of the standard width for the entire expression divided by the width unit for the individual term. To control vertical position, the height of the term with the smallest height is used as the height unit for all terms. The result is an expression that scales to fill the available space as terms of different types are added and removed.

3.3 Affordances for interaction

To keep the focus on the content being presented, interactions need to be intuitive and unencumbered. As previously mentioned, any input on a mobile device can frustrate the user if not well implemented. In the present case, this was handled by trading off between flexibility and ease of interaction. There are only certain parts of the terms and expressions that the user can modify. For example, in a polynomial term with a single variable such as $3x^5$, it does not matter whether the variable is an x or a y. The meaning of the term is the same if the coefficient and the exponent are the same. This means that instead of having three parts to modify, the user only has two. In the display, parts that can be modified are shown using a different color, while static pieces are shown in black.

Another example of limiting flexibility to ease interactivity is in the use of predefined derived classes of MathTerm. This makes sense since mathematics instruction is usually broken down by function type. For example, it is common in calculus to learn polynomial differentiation and then move on to other function types. In the current implementation of the input system, the user is provided with buttons that allow them to add whole terms of a variety of types to their expressions. Then, they can tap various parts of the expression to modify their values. If we consider the entry of the term $3\cos^2(4x)$ using a traditional input system on a mobile device it would take at least 14 screen taps including switching between text, numeric, and symbolic keyboards at least four times. In the present system, entry of this term would take nine screen taps and require no switching between keyboards as a tap on the 3 will bring up a numeric only keyboard and a tap on the cosine functions will bring up a list of trigonometric functions. By knowing which part of the expression is being edited, the number of options can be greatly reduced from a full keyboard layout with ~30 key options to a smaller keyboard with ~10 options. Limiting the number of options reduces the time the user spends searching for the right key.

4. Results

The system developed has been implemented in a mobile game for calculus and physics. This game covers topics including derivatives, integrals, and function behavior. All problems are randomly generated at run time. In addition, the answer is determined and then compared to the user's answer.

Figure 4 shows how a player would complete a problem asking them to find the derivative of a polynomial function. In **Figure 4a**, the initial problem is shown, and the user can use any of the three buttons to insert a polynomial, rational, or trigonometric term, respectively. In **Figure 4b**, the player has inserted two polynomial terms using the polynomial term button. Initially, the coefficients and exponents are not set to values and the player can tap to edit them. Finally, in **Figure 4c**, the player has entered the correct coefficients and exponents and tapped to change the middle operator to a minus. Once the player taps submit, their answer will be checked symbolically. They will be told whether they are correct and be shown the correct answer to the question.

Figure 5 shows (a) an integration problem and (b) an example of how different types of terms scale together so that the sizing of all components is consistent. In **Figure 5a**, the player is asked to find the integral of an expression containing two

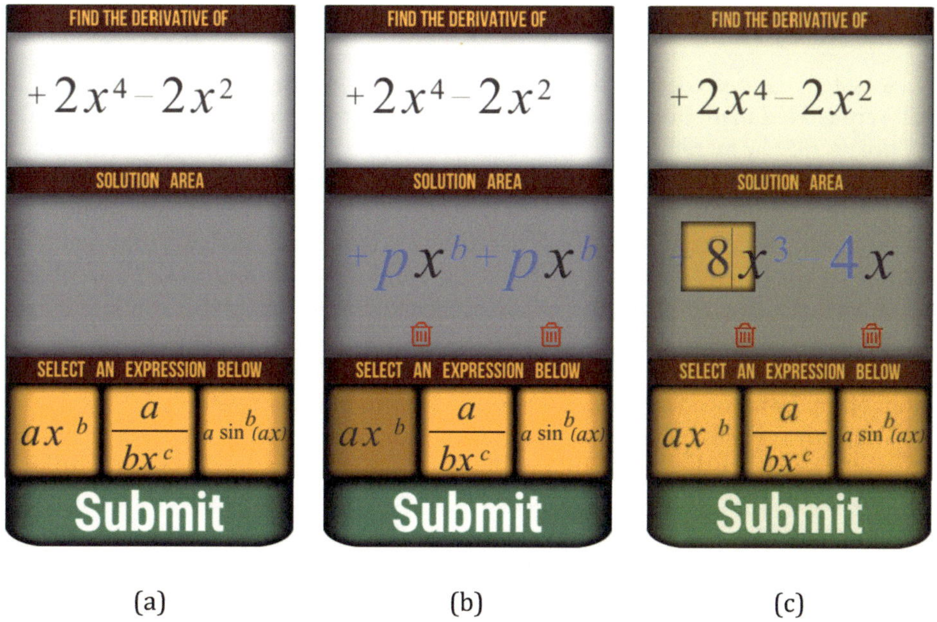

Figure 4.
Derivative problem showing (a) problem statement, (b) after player tapped to include a polynomial term, and (c) after player tapped to add additional term, change a sign and enter coefficients and exponents.

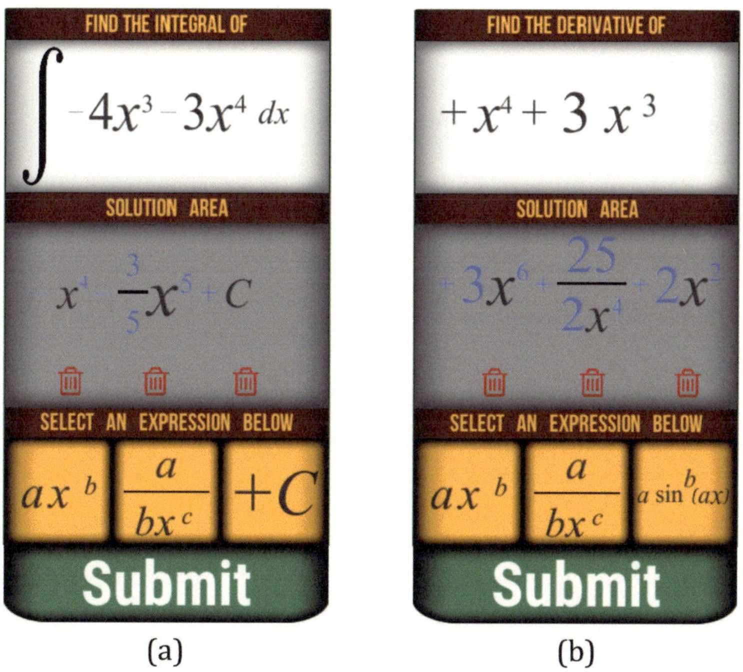

Figure 5.
More examples. (a) Integral question with fractional coefficients and (b) derivative question showing terms scaled as additional terms are added.

polynomial terms. The player has entered two polynomial terms and a constant as their answer. The lead coefficient is converted from a whole number to a fraction by tapping and holding. Then the numerator and denominator can be manipulated individually.

5. Conclusions and future work

A system has been designed and developed that allows mathematical expressions to be embedded in mobile games. This system uses a consistent software design to support symbolic manipulation and display of expressions. This design facilitates reuse even if a different game engine is used by clearly separating the classes used for manipulation from those that implement display. Additionally, spacing and sizing of expression components are controlled to enhance readability and understanding. Finally, affordances are provided to support user interaction. Expressions are constructed by combining template terms and manipulating the components of those terms to provide balance between the desire for players to have the freedom to enter a variety of answers and the complexity, in both manipulation and user interaction, introduced by allowing answer entry to be truly freeform.

There are several directions that can be addressed in future work. First, additional classes can be developed to provide the ability to solve problems with different function types. Also, when the player is presented with a question, the question is on a separate panel which removes the player from game play. It would be better to incorporate the problems more diegetically and incorporate them directly into the scene of the game. Finally, additional affordances for interaction can be included that make interactions even more natural. For example, some players may not find it intuitive to tap and hold to convert a whole number to a fraction. It would be interesting to study this mode of interaction with alternatives, such as swiping up or down, to determine which is most intuitive and provides the best outcomes.

Acknowledgements

This work was made possible through the Office of Naval Research STEM under ONR GRANT11899718.

Conflict of interest

The authors declare no conflict of interest.

Author details

Katherine Smith*, Yuzhong Shen and Anthony Dean
Old Dominion University, Norfolk, Virginia, United States of America

*Address all correspondence to: k3smith@odu.edu

References

[1] Brooks DC. ECAR Study of Undergraduate Students and Information Technology. Louisville, CO: EDUCASE; 2016

[2] Sharples M, Taylor J, Vavoula G. Towards a theory of mobile learning. In: Proceedings of mLearn. 2005

[3] Baya'a NF, Wajeeh DM. Learning mathematics in an authentic mobile environment: The perceptions of students. International Journal of Interactive Mobile Technologies. 2009;**3**:6-14

[4] Lizzio A, Wilson K, Simons R. University students' perceptions of the learning environment and academic outcomes: Implications for theory and practice. Studies in Higher Education. 2002;**27**(1):27-52

[5] Elias T. Universal instructional design principles for mobile learning. The International Review of Research in Open and Distributed Learning. 2011;**12**(2):143-156

[6] Gikas J, Grant MM. Mobile computing devices in higher education: Student perspectives on learning with cellphones, smartphones and social media. The Internet and Higher Education. 2013;**19**:18-26

[7] Nakamura Y, Nakahara T. A new mathematics input interface with flick operation for mobile devices. MSOR Connections. 2016;**15**(2):76-82

[8] Cheon J, Lee S, Crooks S, Song J. An investigation of mobile learning readiness in higher education based on the theory of planned behavior. Computers & Education. 2012;**3**:1054-1064

[9] Watson J, Angus SD. Does regular online testing enhance student learning? Evidence from a large first-year quantitative methods course. In: The Quantitative Analysis of Teaching and Learning in Higher Education in Business, Economics and Commerce: Forum Proceedings. Parkville, VIC, Australia: University of Melbourne; 2008

[10] Lee D, Moon J, Kim YJ, Mun YY. Antecedents and consequences of mobile phone usability: Linking simplicity and interactivity to satisfaction, trust, and brand loyalty. Information and Management. 2015;**52**(3):295-304

[11] Rubin A. Technology Meets Math Education: Envisioning a Practical Future Forum on the Future of Technology in Education. Technical Education Research Centers (TERC); 1999

[12] Williams DL, Boone R, Kingley KV. Eacher beliefs about educational software: A delphi study. Journal of Research on Technology in Education. 2004;**36**(3):213-229

[13] Smith K, Shull J, Dean A, Shen Y, Michaeli J. SiGMA: A software framework for integrating advanced mathematical capabilities in serious game development. Advances in Engineering Software. 2016;**100**:319-325

[14] IXL Learning. IXL Math Online Math Practice [Online]. 2019. Available from: https://www.ixl.com/math [Accessed: 20 May 2019]

[15] Khan Academy. Khan Academy [Online]. 2019. Available from: https://www.khanacademy.org [Accessed: 20 May 2019]

[16] Unity Technologies. Unity [Online]. 2019. Available from: https://unity.com/ [Accessed: 20 May 2019]

[17] Wu W-H, Wu Y-CJ, Chen C-Y, Kao H-Y, Lin C-H, Huang S-H. Review of trends from mobile learning studies: A meta-analysis. Computers & Education. 2012;**59**(2):817-827

Section 2

Evaluation

Chapter 5

Use of Cloud Gaming in Education

Mirko Sužnjević and Maja Homen

Abstract

The use of digital games in education has been the subject of research for many years and their usefulness has been confirmed by many studies and research projects. Standardized tests, such as PISA test, show that respondents achieved better reading, math and physics results if they used the computer more for gaming-related activities. It has been proven that the application of video games in education increases student motivation, improves several types of key skills—social and intellectual skills, reflexes and concentration. Nevertheless, there are several challenges associated with the application of video games in schools and they can be categorized as technical (network and end device limitations), competency (teachers' knowledge in the area), qualitative (lack of educational games of high quality), and financial (high cost of purchasing games and equipment). The novel architecture for delivery of gaming content commonly referred to as "cloud gaming" has the potential to solve most of the present challenges of using games in education. A well-designed cloud gaming platform would enable seamless and simple usage for both students and teachers. While solving most of the present problems, cloud gaming introduces a set of new research challenges which will be discussed in this section.

Keywords: cloud gaming, education, video games, quality of experience, optimization

1. Introduction

It is very important that the establishment of ICT infrastructure in schools be supported by the introduction of services that will use this infrastructure, which is shown on the example of Turkey [1, 2], which introduced such infrastructure to schools without innovative services and has not yielded significant results in the improvement of the educational process. Using games in schools is one of the innovative services that can drive motivation of students for better participation and make the schools happier places for all children.

The use of digital games in education has been the subject of research for many years and their usefulness has been confirmed by research [3–6]. Although the potential for learning through video games is great, the instances of application of this learning methodology so far have been rare. The basic challenges associated with the application of video games in schools are divided into technical (e.g., end device limitations), competency (e.g., teachers' knowledge in the area), qualitative (e.g., few educational games of high quality), and financial (e.g., high cost of purchasing games) [7]. Besides the listed issues, for games to be adopted and incorporated in formal education, policies would have to be made by the key stakeholders in all sections of the society, such as in education, government, independent and standardization bodies, and the game industry.

Cloud gaming provides a new concept of online games organization, where the game is completely stored and played on a server located on a cloud. A high-definition video is sent to the client, and user commands are sent to the server. The cloud gaming concept has the potential to solve most of the above problems because it does not require a powerful client device (mobile devices are sufficient), does not require any additional competency from the teachers (games are located in the cloud), enables the use of the newest and most graphically advanced games, and reduces the number of required licenses. Therefore, the use of cloud gaming for delivering gaming content in educational environment could be a solution which would enable all the benefits while removing the major downsides and challenges. Nevertheless, this concept brings a series of research challenges related to optimization of interactive video streaming based on available computing and network resources with the goal of maximizing overall Quality of Experience (QoE). Also, there is always a question of appropriate content for each of the educational units defined by the curriculum, as well as the problem of adapting the existing and designing new games while bearing in mind the diversity of delivery platforms on which they can be played (primarily tablets and mobile phones). The interdisciplinary nature of this research area requires an approach that will combine technical research with social research in the field of educational application of advanced technical tools.

The remainder of the chapter is organized as follows. In Section 2, an overview of advantages and current issues of using video games as a teaching tool is presented. Cloud gaming is described in detail in Section 3. Section 4 presents the discussion on the problems of using games in schools and how cloud gaming could solve these problems, also discussing which research problems need to be overcome if cloud gaming is to be used as a platform for games as a teaching tool. Section 5 presents the roadmap of research efforts needed to solve the identified research problems.

2. Using games as a teaching tool: an overview of advantages and issues

The use of digital games in education has been the subject of research for many years and their usefulness has been confirmed by research [3–6]. Standardized tests, such as PISA test, show that respondents achieved better reading, math and physics results if they used the computer more for gaming-related activities [8]. Newest research [9, 10] also confirmed that digital games can improve communication skills, adaptability and resourcefulness in elementary school students and even in university students [11]. Social games in education are becoming increasingly relevant because they can provide solutions to certain problems seen in traditional school environments, for example, lower cognitive outcomes and poor attitudes towards learning. Video games require students to challenge themselves, collaborate and interact with peers and they promote critical thinking. All of those skills are necessary for students to thrive in today's digital world [12]. Previous research showed that with collaborative games students can learn and practice social skills and the games can improve their engagement in the classroom. Social skills are important because they are tied to peer and teacher acceptance as well as academic achievement [13]. Social games embed various communication possibilities and levels of interaction between students; thus, different types of learners can enjoyably engage with contents of learning in a familiar and fun way. Digital game-based learning and academic achievement are closely related: students who are more motivated to perform better at games are also more motivated to achieve better academic results. There is a connection between skill mastery, progression and rewards both in gaming and in education contexts [14].

There is a special field of research regarding serious (learning) games. Serious games are designed for other purposes than pure entertainment. They are used in many areas such as; education, healthcare, marketing, engineering etc. Serious game-based approach to learning can be used in many different curricular areas and newest research showed that it promotes better learning and students' motivation and enjoyment [15, 16]. Serious games proved to be an especially great tool when it comes to general problem-solving skills [17], language learning [18–20], history and physical education [20] as well as science education [18, 21, 22]. Games have also been researched in special needs education students and research showed that using serious games in education enhances students' cognitive outcomes as well as social behavior [23–25].

Like every other method, the usage of serious games for learning has some advantages and disadvantages. Combination of the relative novelty of the whole field and the general breakneck pace at which the gaming industry is developing produces various difficulties in evaluation of results. The lack of methodological standards when it comes to using digital games in education also makes it hard to directly compare the results of different studies. Additionally, research in the field is often focused more on the effects in specific fields of education (health industry, military or corporate training, etc.) and less on the impact on formal education as such.

With the soaring costs and complexities of developing digital games at large, such educational projects are also in great danger of being abandoned unfinished; with the tendency of modern video games to be in perpetual development cycles, sometimes it is hard to even get a finished product in this field. That level of constant change can make it impossible to properly evaluate the educational impact of a game and isolate important factors for research purposes.

The research into negative sides of digital games is also a contentious subject, which can make it hard to filter out the potential bias in available results. So, while the positive side of serious games as an educational tool is unquestionably promising, further research into potential disadvantages is certainly warranted.

Large number of research projects in the area of using games as a teaching tool was conducted in the recent years, which was summed up and evaluated in a European Schoolnet study [7]. The main conclusions of the study were that the application of video games in schools increases student motivation, improves several types of key skills—social and intellectual skills, reflexes and concentration. Several analyzed projects also show increased knowledge about the subjects taught. Increased mathematical knowledge was demonstrated in DANT and The Consolarium projects [26]. Through its research institute, the Joint Research Centre, the European Union has studied the possibility of using video games in education as well as reducing the risk of exclusion of vulnerable groups [7, 11], and it finances projects related to the use of video games in education. The Gaming Horizons project studied the role of digital games in culture, education and economy. The final report stated that video games can create new learning opportunities that are more focused on the student, thanks to their motivational capacity and motivational strength [27]. The objective of the InLife project was to create a new gaming framework in education that would exploit the new concept of the Internet of things as well as educational digital games. The current phase of research in this field in the European Union is medium and large studies in schools funded through projects of the member states or the European Union.

3. Cloud gaming

3.1 Technical overview

Cloud gaming provides a new concept of online games organization, where the game is delivered from a server located in a cloud. According to [28], the most important and currently most implemented model for cloud gaming is "Remote Rendering Gaming as a Service", in which the multiplayer server, the game logic, and the rendering are all located on the server, while the only main functionality left to the client is the input module. In this model a high-definition video is sent to the client and user commands are sent to the server. The cloud gaming concept is illustrated in **Figure 1**. The user commands are sent from the user devices and the high definition video stream is sent from the cloud gaming server to the users. The traffic is highly asymmetrical as the high definition video flow is much more demanding in terms of network bandwidth than the user commands.

The advantage of this approach is that only video content is displayed on the client's device and that all games are played through the same client application. This computationally less demanding functionality is generally supported by mobile devices, and it is independent of the operating system of the client's device. Therefore, the client does not have to employ the most recent, expensive hardware equipment to be able to play the newest, often very resource hungry games. The most conspicuous disadvantage is that the client has to be connected to a network that has a very high bandwidth (one stream goes up to 50 Mbit/s) and very low network latency (less than 70 ms of Round-Trip Time). Conventional methods of reducing the effects of poor network conditions on the multi-media content streaming (such as temporary storage of data in buffer until they are ready for display or precoding the video in different formats) cannot be applied in this case, because they introduce additional latency into the system and due to the fact that the video does not exist before the user defines it with their controls. Latency in the cloud gaming system reduces its interactivity and the Quality of Experience (QoE) of the end user. There are a number of studies focusing on the impact of latency on the QoE of the user, but in general cloud gaming systems require less than 70 ms on Round Trip Time network latency (e.g., GeForce NOW).

The estimated net worth of global cloud gaming market in 2018 was $ 802 million, while it is estimated to reach up to $ 6.944 billion in the year 2026 according to

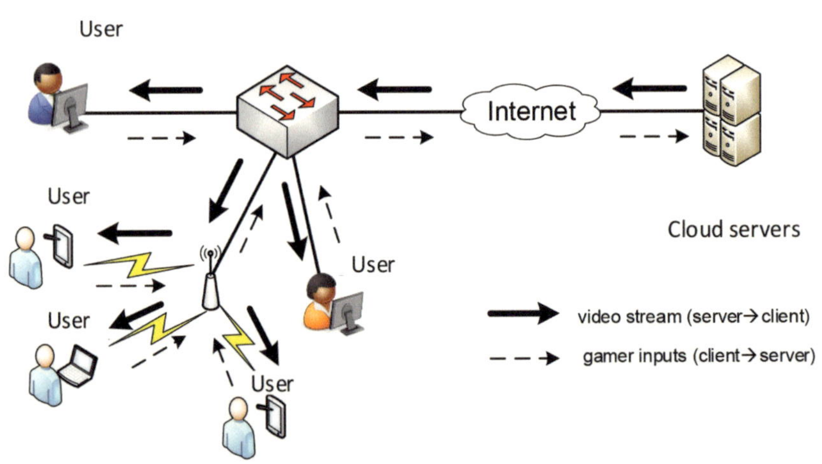

Figure 1.
Cloud gaming architecture.

the Zion market research [29]. The market is very competitive and the first services Gaikai and OnLive were unsuccessful on the market and were acquired by Sony in 2012 and 2015 respectively. Some of the main technical issues that led to shutting down of the pioneers of cloud gaming were problems with the virtualization of the Graphics Processing Unit (GPU) and insufficient penetration of the high broadband Internet connections (10 Mbit/s and more). Sony's PlayStation NOW is powered by the technology developed by Gaika. There are currently several commercial platforms for cloud gaming on the market, such as GeForceNOW, G-Cluster, PlayKey.net, Parsec, Vortex, etc. This field is very propulsive and even some of the largest companies on the ICT market, such as Microsoft and Google, announced their Xcloud and Stadia platforms.

3.2 Research challenges in the area of cloud gaming

The research field is very dynamic and deals with the following key issues: (1) virtualization of graphic resources [30–32], (2) new video encoding methods adapted to the needs of highly interactive applications [33–35] and (3) the optimization of the QoE based on available resources, whether they are network related [36, 37], related to the game type [38] or related to the distribution of virtual machines [39]. One of the main research problems in cloud gaming is optimization of the end user's QoE taking into account the available server, client, and primarily network resources. For that to be done, the first QoE models need to be derived from detailed user studies. We describe in detail the related work in this area.

User studies are the first and basic step in the modeling of the QoE of any service. The factors affecting the QoE can be divided into systemic, user and contextual [40]. Most of the studies in this field focused on the impact of network latency and loss of package on the QoE [41–48]. In general, the results show that cloud gaming is highly sensitive to network latency and that package losses of less than 1% caused significant degradation of the players' QoE [40], as confirmed by a commercial platform study [49], but also by a study of an open-source platform GamingAnywhere [50]. The research clearly recognized the sensitivity of this service to network degradation and it is therefore necessary to dynamically adjust the service to network condition on the basis of optimization of algorithms in order to avoid congestion that causes latency and package losses. Although various media is sent in the concept of cloud gaming, most of the network traffic is generated by video streaming [51], which is the key optimization medium. One of the video encoding methods that exploits the specific features of cloud gaming is the cooperative encoding of videos of different users in the same session to take advantage of the established redundancy between their videos [52]. This method has the potential for application in the educational environment, because in this scenario all the students in a class play the same video game. Defining the players' area of interest within the scene and the different encoding of scenes detail at macroblocks level is a method by which significant savings can be achieved in the used network traffic, while retaining a high level of the QoE [53]. A similar principle of interest field analysis is used in [54], but by using virtual scene rendering information, which enables acceleration of the video encoding process, especially the calculation of the motion vector and selection of the macroblock mode, which reduces encoding time by as much as 72%. Although compression can reduce the amount of data being sent, the variable state of the network can lead to instability of the service and the decrease of the QoE. For the system to be adaptable to network parameters variations (primary bandwidth and latency), optimization mechanisms and adaptive video streaming are required. The basic principle in such optimizations is that interactivity is the most important component of video games and that video quality is secondary, within certain limits of course, as well as that video encoding parameters can be adapted to enable adaptive video streaming [55]. The optimization of video streaming based on the network latency is presented in [56] and a special package distribution scheme for the transmission of cloud video streams is presented in [34]. A review article [57] sums up research in this field and open research problems. All reviewed papers deal with the issues of using cloud gaming in an entertaining context. The scenario of application in the educational environment opens up many new research questions and optimization opportunities; to the best of our knowledge, there have been no studies dealing with education as a specific case study so far.

4. How cloud gaming solves issues in using games as a teaching tool?

Like in many other countries, in Croatia the problem of outdatedness of the teaching methodology applied in schools has been recognized, and the Strategy of Education, Science and Technology defines that it is necessary to "develop digital educational contents, tools and methods of using ICT in learning and teaching." [58]. The increase in the number and availability of mobile devices has created predispositions for introducing digital education through gaming in schools, and mobile tablet devices have recently often been mentioned as a potential replacement for paper textbooks in schools. Some of the advantages of mobile tablet devices over the textbooks include: faster learning [59], reduction of physical load on children who are overloaded with the weight of textbooks [60], the availability of a large number of textbooks in digital form, new approaches to learning and more. Using games in schools can be one of the steps on the road towards the goal of reaching advanced digital education. Nevertheless, for this step to be taken in practice, significant challenges need to be overcome.

As we previously stated, the basic challenges associated with the application of video games in schools are divided into ***technical, competency, qualitative and financial*** [7].

- One of the main **technical problems** in the integration of contemporary video games in classrooms is that newer games require that the graphics processor performs a large number of demanding computing operations in real time, and most of the graphics processors built into mobile devices do not have enough processor power to achieve this task. The heterogeneity of tablet devices in terms of operating systems and technical features (e.g. display size, storage, processor speed) is also a problem. Additionally, games today require a lot of storage space on the hard disc (e.g., the newest Call of Duty Modern Warfare requires 175 GB of disc space), which severely limits the number and quality of the games which can be played.

- **Competency problems** relate to teachers and the lack of information on using video games in teaching and the question of which games to use in relation to which teaching material. Additionally, in "classic" computer classrooms, teachers have the major burden of maintaining the ICT structure in both hardware and, especially, software aspect—for which teachers do not have quality competencies or sufficient time.

- The **quality problems** are related to the lack of appropriate educational games, which are mostly significantly inferior to games that are developed exclusively for entertainment purposes [61]. Also, the technical aspect of games being developed for a particular platform and operating system fragments the pool of existing educational games with high quality to further extent. For example, a game developed for PC and therefore usually Windows operating system cannot be played on a tablet.

- **Financial problems** include the cost of purchasing one game per device, which could be a major burden to school budgets. The cost could be very high if multiple games could only be used in a single course. Additionally, there are rather weak financial justifications for the development of serious games—the market is far smaller and harder to reach, while the lack of information and sorry design of the games are hindering market development. In order to support as many mobile devices as possible, game developers need to develop multiple versions of a game for different platforms (e.g. *ios* and Android operating systems), which increases costs, and they are further limited by the heterogeneous technical features of devices.

Cloud gaming concept has the potential to solve most of the above problems by the way it is designed. Here we list how the major problems in introducing games in classrooms are completely solved or partially alleviated:

- Technical problems:
    - *Processing power*—this issue is completely solved because only reproduction of the video stream and capturing of the user's input is required, and those functions impose very low processing load.
    - *Heterogeneity of user devices* and their processor power are solved as the overwhelming majority of smartphones and tablets in the market are capable of reproducing a video stream with no issues. Therefore, any of these devices is capable of serving as a cloud gaming client device.
    - *Storage space*—the games are stored on the cloud and the video stream received on the client side is discarded after being displayed. The client application which displays the streaming video and captures the input from the user has relatively low storage requirements (e.g., installation package for open source cloud gaming platform GamingAnywhere is a bit smaller than 8 MB).
- Competency problems:
    - *Maintaining the IT infrastructure*—teachers do not have to maintain the IT infrastructure because games are stored on a cloud, so only one application per user device needs to be installed. Therefore, problems can only arise with running one application and not multiple ones, so any troubleshooting would require much less effort;
    - *Appropriate games*—This issue is not solved by the cloud gaming approach per se, but a centralized nature of the cloud gaming system enables the implementation of a recommended system for a particular lesson. The more details on what such a solution would require is given in the next section.
- Quality problems:
    - *Fragmentation of the appropriate educational games*—cloud gaming approach enables playing the games which are designed for any platform on any other

platform. If a game is developed for Windows, the virtual machine in the cloud on which the game is run needs to have a Windows operating system, but the client machine can run any operating system, for example Android or iOS.

- *Lack of high-quality educational games*—cloud gaming system enables the use of high-quality games which were designed for entertainment purposes in educational context (e.g., using one of the games from Civilization series to teach history).

- Financial problems:

  - *Cost of game purchasing*—the cloud gaming platform allows for a large number of students to use the same game license under the conditions negotiated with the game developer, of course.

  - *Costs of developing educational games*—the cost for developers is reduced because they need to develop the game for only one platform.

  - *Market size*—deploying a cloud gaming platform which would serve as a country-wide enabler of games in schools opens up a large market, which would be an incentive for game developers. If successful, such approach could be followed by other countries or stakeholders, which would further expand the market.

As presented, cloud gaming offers the potential to completely or partially solve listed problems, but also brings a series of challenges for application in schools in order to make it successful. In the next section we describe the research challenges which need to be overcome for this goal to be achieved.

4.1 Cloud gaming in teaching: research problems

The case study of using cloud gaming in classrooms has its own specific user and technical requirements and limitations (e.g., the number of users sharing wireless network, background traffic, same game etc.). In order to solve them, the cooperation of researchers in the technical and educational field is necessary. It is necessary to evaluate the knowledge and expectations of students as well as teachers, identify technical characteristics of traffic and traffic infrastructure, create models that optimize the QoE depending on dynamically changing network resources, study the existing games that can be used for educational purposes and define the methodology for adding new games, optimize video streaming on the server side, evaluate the system and refine it based on feedback from end users – teachers and students. An additional challenge is that the data transfer in the last step is performed via wireless networks that have lower performance than wired networks. **Figure 2** illustrates the functionality of the cloud gaming concept with application in education as well as open research questions in both technical and educational area.

4.2 Technical research problems

The technical research problems are mostly related to the infrastructure constraints on the server and the network side, as well as how to enable best possible QoE of end users given the said constraints. Besides that, on the user side there is a problem of designing an appropriate interface or interface modifications which would enable playing a game.

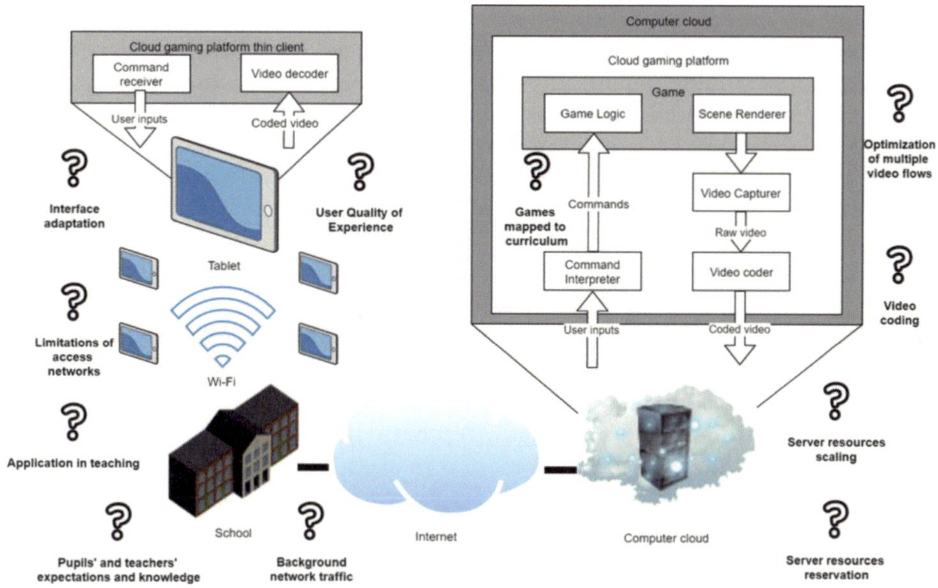

Figure 2.
Research questions related to the cloud gaming concept with application in education.

In the ideal scenario a whole class would be able to play a game which their teacher has instructed them to. With 30 students in class and 30 Mbit/s of generated traffic per game stream this yields 900 Mbit/s of overall traffic load. All this traffic must first go through a wireless network (preferably WiFi) and through the school network towards the cloud in which the servers are stored. In Croatia the schools which were connected to the Internet within the e-schools project are connected with the main Carnet network via high speed optical links and those backbone links should not be a problem for cloud gaming traffic. Nevertheless, the problem might arise if these links get overloaded with other types of background network traffic; therefore, an overall **analysis of network traffic** traversing these links is needed. The results of such analysis are needed to properly dimension the cloud gaming network flows depending on the number of users. The bigger network issue is the WiFi connectivity as a bottleneck. The latest WiFi standard IEEE 802.11ax [62] is promised to have speeds up to 10 Gbit/s, which might solve the issues of bottleneck on this section, but the current most popular standard offers up to 1.3 Gbits/s in theory, which is in practice limited up to a half of the value depending on the strength of the signal, the number of devices connected, other networks etc. Therefore, an **analysis of capabilities of current WiFi standard 802.11ac for serving multiple cloud gaming flows** is needed. Previous standards showed little potential for such application as the QoE of the end user was severely degraded when only five users were using the service [63].

Because of the limitations of the infrastructure and fluctuating background traffic, there is a need for an **optimization algorithm for adapting the characteristics of video streams** in a way which would maximize the end users' QoE under the current constraints. For the optimization to be possible, first the **QoE models for the games** which are used in the educational settings need to be devised. There has been significant research in the QoE of games used in entertainment context for cloud gaming and "regular" network gaming. These results can serve as a basis for devising the QoE models for games in educational context, but further research is needed because of a different context which may have a significant impact on the QoE.

Finally, the current generation of general-purpose video codecs has not been developed with a cloud gaming in mind. Bandwidth and especially latency constraints of cloud gaming impose additional requirements on the video codec, but specifics of the application offer possibilities for **advanced video coding methods**, which could speed up the coding process, lower the bandwidth required, or even lower the latency by pre-coding different outcomes, which can happen based on user input, and basically "predicting the future" [35].

4.3 Educational research problems

First and foremost, in order to make the system useful to end users, it is necessary to examine the opinions and attitudes of teachers and students on the use of videogames in classroom and determine their need for such a system for the sake of its optimal implementation. Teachers should be familiar with the system and know how to make the best of it in class. The system should not be complicated to use.

Regarding videogames, there is a problem that the market lacks serious games, while the existing games should be studied and categorized in detail. Such games could be categorized according to the genre, but the most important categorization would be done according to learning outcomes in specific areas, i.e. mathematics, science, language learning, etc. It is also important to connect the games to the public curriculum in order to make them practical.

As mentioned, there is a significant lack of serious games that could be used in class; therefore, it would be wise to create own games, which would be created for the existing teaching curriculum and in the local language. It would be crucial to include teachers and students in the very process of making of serious games. The needs and demands of end users (students) of serious games ought to be met during the process of their making. The attitudes of educators towards serious games have a significant impact on their adoption in teaching [64]; that is why their inclusion in the process of making of games is of vital importance. In order to make that happen, it is necessary to study different processes of game designing, while giving teachers and students a role in the process of game creation. This could be done through a process of co-creation of games, meaning that all representative members would have their say in the design. This could be realized through various workshops, where teachers and students would participate in the process of game design with the help of different creative tools such as collage, clay, various painting techniques, making of prototypes, storyboards, etc., with game designers and programmers guiding the entire process of game design. Many teaching education faculties have ICT departments that work on the creation of educational packages, which creates a possibility for a productive cooperation.

Mutual design made by teachers and students could transform serious games in education, both through innovation of game content with the examples from teaching curriculum and with the acceptance of games as part of the teaching process. This would make end users co-owners of such games by giving them an important role in their design, creation and, eventually, their use.

5. Cloud gaming in teaching: roadmap of required research

The interdisciplinary nature of the research problem requires an approach that will combine technical and social research in the field of educational application of advanced technical tools. The goal of the presented roadmap is to create a SErver Platform for ClOud Gaming (SEPCOG) with specific purpose for streaming games in the classroom, as well as to devise a methodology for adding appropriate content to the platform. The content may be newly developed, or the existing content could be adapted. We propose an approach composed of the sets of basic research activities illustrated in **Figure 3**.

The first step in this research would be to define a system specification based on the information collected from teachers and students. This data can be collected through surveys of students and teachers. Data collected by surveys may be in the form of responses to questions, as well as free responses. Likert scale might be used to measure the opinions and attitudes of teachers and students and such data would be analyzed by statistical methods.

The second step is to identify the test games which can be used. Available educational or entertainment games could be reviewed with a special emphasis on games in the native language of the country or those that can be localized. The research question is how to identify an educational game and a commercial game that could be used in the educational context, as defined in [61, 65].

A possible scenario for creation of test games would be a joint developing of the game between teachers and students. Such a scenario may be based on a game development system that would be simple enough for children to use. The games for e.g. understanding physical phenomena, mathematical games and the like could be generated under this scenario. For all these approaches in games creation, a methodology for mapping the games according to the units of the existing curriculum ought to be created. The methodology needs to be based on the identification of the learning outcomes of gaming scenarios and the establishing of non-unique relations to the teaching units. This is a major research question that requires careful consideration, which is highly dependent on the country and its educational process. To achieve this objective, a research related to educational content—games that would be streamed as video content to students—needs to be conducted. Available video games of various categories ought to be analyzed. First, test video games that can be used in laboratory research need to be defined. At this point, teachers and their expertise in didactics will be crucial for the success, as well as cooperation between teachers and researchers from technical areas.

The third step needs to be an iterative subjective laboratory testing of the QoE depending on the network parameters and video encoding parameters, as well as the adjustment of the developed system based on the results of these tests. For this research to be carried out, characteristics of the network in schools and the network

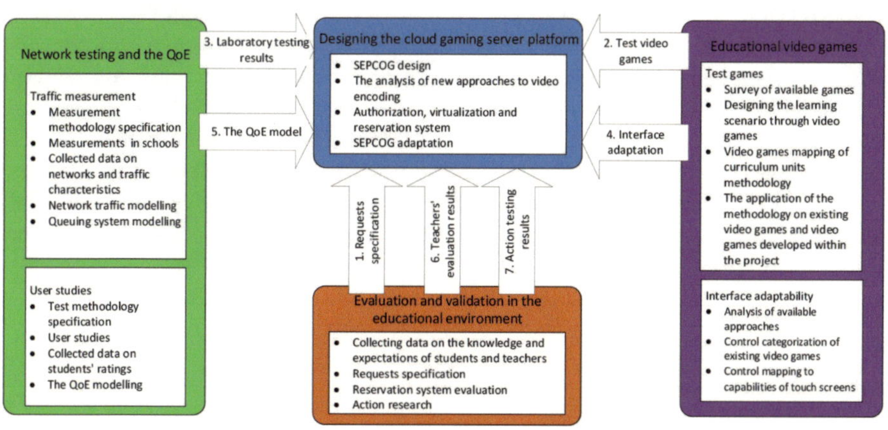

Figure 3.
Research methodology.

traffic have to be identified. Also, the methodology for measuring network traffic in schools has to be specified.

The fourth step needs to be the research of the adjustment of the games' interface to the limitations of the tablet interface (that neither has a keyboard nor a mouse). Today's mobile devices host different types of games, even games that are highly demanding in terms of interaction, such as shooting games. The control methods used in these games can be directly replicated for the needs of cloud gaming, but for that approach a detailed review of the field has to be performed, all valid control methods have to be identified, and the appropriate ones have to be selected. In addition, it is necessary to make a general classification of the interaction of games on PCs and to copy it to touch screen capabilities. Such a research effort needs to be done in accordance with both teachers and students. To achieve this, a methodology for the adaptation of video games to the limitations of mobile device interfaces is needed. The study of methodologies for learning via games development as well as developing own games in cooperation with students is also needed. The development of a methodology for mapping the educational content to the units of the existing curriculum and grouping the educational content according to the teaching units of target subjects is required.

The fifth step which is needed for the validation of the approach is action research—deployment of the developed system in testing schools for teachers and students to use it. Questionnaires have to be specified to identify the main advantages and disadvantages of the developed system by using text encoding and statistical analysis. The aim of the teachers' evaluation is to ensure easy use of the system, while experimental action research is an activity within which the system is handed over to users (teachers and students) in their own environment (classroom) with instructions. At the end of use, researchers should collect data from teachers and students through questionnaires and interviews. Data analysis can be done by statistical and text encoding methods to identify key challenges in the functioning of the system. Once all of these research steps have been conducted, the results implemented in practice could enable a happier and more motivated school attendance of students.

6. Conclusion

In this chapter we have presented a literature review proving the advantages of using digital games in schools, discussed the problems of using games as a teaching tool in practice, and presented the solution based on cloud gaming. We showed that while the advantages are clear, there are significant challenges in applying the use of digital games in schools in practice. We present a possible solution based on the concept of cloud gaming—streaming of live game video to end users' devices, whose video is created in real time based on the results of user commands. We showcase how the cloud gaming approach solves the number of current issues, but we also define research problems which this approach poses. We present a detailed roadmap of the research which needs to be conducted in cooperation of educational and technical research.

Author details

Mirko Sužnjević[1]* and Maja Homen[2]

1 Faculty of Electrical Engineering and Computing, University of Zagreb, Zagreb, Croatia

2 Faculty of Teacher Education, University of Zagreb, Zagreb, Croatia

*Address all correspondence to: mirko.suznjevic@fer.hr

References

[1] Slivar I, Skorin-Kapov L, Suznjevic M. QoE-aware resource allocation for multiple cloud gaming users sharing a bottleneck link. In: 2019 22nd Conference on Innovation in Clouds, Internet and Networks and Workshops (ICIN); February 2019; IEEE. 2019. pp. 118-123

[2] Isci TG, Demir SB. The use of tablets distributed within the scope of FATIH project for education in Turkey (is FATIH project a fiasco or a technological revolution?). Universal Journal of Educational Research. 2015;**3**(7):442-450

[3] Squire K. Video games in education. International Journal of Intelligent Games & Simulation. 2003;**2**(1):49-62

[4] Van Eck R. Digital game-based learning: It's not just the digital natives who are restless. EDUCAUSE Review. 2006;**41**(2):16

[5] Charsky D, Mims C. Integrating commercial off-the-shelf video games into school curriculums. TechTrends. 2008;**52**(5):38-44

[6] Duncan I, Miller A, Jiang S. A taxonomy of virtual worlds usage in education. British Journal of Educational Technology. 2012;**43**(6):949-964

[7] Wastiau P, Kearney C, Van den Berghe W. How Are Digital Games Used in Schools. Brussels: European Schoolnet; 2009

[8] Biagi F, Loi M. Measuring ICT use and learning outcomes: Evidence from recent econometric studies. European Journal of Education. 2013;**48**(1):28-42

[9] Clark DB, Tanner-Smith EE, Killingsworth SS. Digital games, design, and learning: A systematic review and meta-analysis. Review of Educational Research. 2016;**86**(1):79-122

[10] Hamari J, Shernoff DJ, Rowe E, Coller B, Asbell-Clarke J, Edwards T. Challenging games help students learn: An empirical study on engagement, flow and immersion in game-based learning. Computers in Human Behaviour. 2016;**54**:170-179

[11] Barr M. Video games can develop graduate skills in higher education students: A randomised trial. Computers in Education. 2017;**113**:86-97

[12] Marsh J. Purposes for literacy in children's use of the online virtual world Club Penguin. Journal of Research in Reading. 2014;**37**(2):179-195

[13] Lane KL, Menzies HM, Barton-Arwood SM, Doukas GL, Munton SM. Designing, implementing, and evaluating social skills interventions for elementary students: Step-by-step procedures based on actual school-based investigations. Preventing School Failure: Alternative Education for Children and Youth. 2005;**49**(2):18-26

[14] Heeter C, Lee YH, Medler B, Magerko B. Beyond player types: Gaming achievement goal. In: Taylor TL, editor. Proceedings of the 2011 ACM SIGGRAPH Symposium on Video Games. 2011. pp. 43-47. DOI: 10.1145/2018556.2018565

[15] Lamb R, Annetta L, Firestone J. A meta-analysis with examination of moderators of student cognition, affect, and learning outcomes while using serious educational games, serious games, and simulations. Computers in Human Behavior. 2018;**80**:158-167. DOI: 10.1016/j.chb.2017.10.040

[16] Garneli V, Giannakos M, Chorianopoulos K. Serious games as a malleable learning medium: The effects of narrative, gameplay, and making on students' performance and

attitudes. British Journal of Educational Technology. 2017;**48**(3):842-859

[17] Monroy C, Klisch Y, Miller L. Emerging contexts for science education: Embedding a forensic science game in a virtual world. In: Bruce H, Grudin J, editors. Proceedings of the 2011 iConference. New York: ACM; 2011. pp. 622-629. Retrieved from: http://dl.acm.org/citation.cfm?id=1940845

[18] Mayer R. What should be the role of computer games in education? Policy Insights From the Behavioral and Brain Sciences. 2016;**3**:20-26. DOI: 10.1177/2372732215621311

[19] Berns A, Isla-Montes JL, Palomo-Duarte M, Dodero JM. Motivation, students' needs and learning outcomes: A hybrid game-based app for enhanced language learning. Springerplus. 2016;**5**(1):1305

[20] Young MF, Slota S, Cutter AB, Jalette G, Mullin G, Lai B, et al. Our princess is in another castle: A review of trends in serious gaming for education. Review of Educational Research. 2012;**82**(1):61-89

[21] Hakulinen L. Using serious games in computer science education. In: Simon A, Kinnunen P, editors. Proceedings of the 11th Koli Calling International Conference on Computing Education Research—Koli Calling. Vol. 11. 2011. pp. 83-88

[22] Cheng MT, Chen JH, Chu SJ, et al. The use of serious games in science education: A review of selected empirical research from 2002 to 2013. Journal of Computers in Education. 2015;**2**:353-375. DOI: 10.1007/s40692-015-0039-9

[23] Bakker M, van den Heuvel-Panhuizen M, Robitzsch A. Effects of mathematics computer games on special education students' multiplicative reasoning ability. British Journal of Educational Technology. 2016;**47**(4):633-648

[24] Durkin K, Boyle J, Hunter S, Conti-Ramsden G. Video games for children and adolescents with special educational needs. Zeitschrift Für Psychologie. 2013;**221**(2):79-89. DOI: 10.1027/2151-2604/a000138

[25] Karal H, Kokoç M, Ayyıldız U. Educational computer games for developing psychomotor ability in children with mild mental impairment. Procedia—Social and Behavioral Sciences. 2010;**9**:996-1000

[26] Groff J, Howells C, Cranmer S. Console game-based pedagogy: A study of primary and secondary classroom learning through console video games. International Journal of Game-Based Learning. 2012;**2**(2):35-54

[27] Persico D, Bailey C, Buijtenweg TP, Dagnino FM, Earp J, Haggis-Burridge M, et al. Gaming horizons deliverable D 1.8. Gaming horizons: Alternative framings for a new role of gaming in education and society: Deliverables. In: Final Research Report. Breda University; 2018

[28] Cai W, Chen M, Leung VC. Toward gaming as a service. IEEE Internet Computing. 2014;**18**(3):12-18

[29] Zion Market Research. Global Cloud Gaming Market Will Reach USD 6,944 Million By 2026: Zion Market Research [Internet]. 2018. Available from: https://www.globenewswire.com/news-release/2018/12/31/1679151/0/en/Global-Cloud-Gaming-Market-Will-Reach-USD-6-944-Million-By-2026-Zion-Market-Research.html

[30] Shea R, Liu J. On GPU pass-through performance for cloud gaming: Experiments and analysis. In: Proceedings of Annual Workshop on Network and Systems Support for Games. IEEE Press; 2013. pp. 1-6

[31] Zhao Z, Hwang K, Villeta J. Game cloud design with virtualized CPU/GPU servers and initial performance results. In: Proceedings of the 3rd Workshop on Scientific Cloud Computing; ACM. 2012. pp. 23-30

[32] Qi Z, Yao J, Zhang C, Yu M, Yang Z, Guan H. VGRIS: Virtualized GPU resource isolation and scheduling in cloud gaming. ACM Transactions on Architecture and Code Optimization (TACO). 2014;**11**(2):17

[33] Shi S, Hsu CH, Nahrstedt K, Campbell R. Using graphics rendering contexts to enhance the real-time video coding for mobile cloud gaming. In: Proceedings of the 19th ACM International Conference on Multimedia; ACM. 2011, 2011. pp. 103-112

[34] Wu J, Yuen C, Cheung NM, Chen J, Chen CW. Enabling adaptive high-frame-rate video streaming in mobile cloud gaming applications. IEEE Transactions on Circuits and Systems for Video Technology. 2015;**25**(12):1988-2001

[35] Lee K, Chu D, Cuervo E, Kopf J, Degtyarev Y, Grizan S, et al. Outatime: Using speculation to enable low-latency continuous interaction for mobile cloud gaming. In: Proceedings of the 13th Annual International Conference on Mobile Systems, Applications, and Services; ACM. 2015. pp. 151-165

[36] Jarschel M, Schlosser D, Scheuring S, Hoßfeld T. An evaluation of QoE in cloud gaming based on subjective tests. In: 2011 Fifth International Conference on Innovative Mobile and Internet Services in Ubiquitous Computing; June 2011; IEEE. 2011, 2011. pp. 330-335

[37] Lee YT, Chen KT, Su HI, Lei CL. Are all games equally cloud-gaming-friendly?: An electromyographic approach. In: Proceedings of the 11th Annual Workshop on Network and Systems Support for Games; November 2012; IEEE Press. 2012, 2011. p. 3

[38] Jarschel M, Schlosser D, Scheuring S, Hoßfeld T. Gaming in the clouds: QoE and the users' perspective. Mathematical and Computer Modelling. 2013;**57**(11-12):2883-2894

[39] Hong HJ, Chen DY, Huang CY, Chen KT, Hsu CH. QoE-aware virtual machine placement for cloud games. In: 2013 12th Annual Workshop on Network and Systems Support for Games (NetGames); December 2013; IEEE. 2013, 2013. pp. 1-2

[40] Clincy V, Wilgor B. Subjective evaluation of latency and packet loss in a cloud-based game. In: 2013 10th International Conference on Information Technology: New Generations; April 2013; IEEE. 2013. pp. 473-476

[41] Slivar I, Suznjevic M, Skorin-Kapov L, Matijasevic M. Empirical QoE study of in-home streaming of online games. In: 2014 13th Annual Workshop on Network and Systems Support for Games; December 2014; IEEE. 2014. pp. 1-6

[42] Brunnström K, Beker SA, De Moor K, Dooms A, Egger S, Garcia MN, et al. Qualinet White Paper on Definitions of Quality of Experience. Novi Sad: European Network on Quality of Experience in Multimedia Systems and Services (COST Action IC 1003); 2013

[43] Claypool M, Finkel D. The effects of latency on player performance in cloud-based games. In: 2014 13th Annual Workshop on Network and Systems Support for Games; ; December 2014; IEEE. 2014. pp. 1-6

[44] Liu Y, Wang S, Dey S. Content-aware modeling and enhancing user experience in cloud mobile rendering and streaming. IEEE Journal on

Emerging and Selected Topics in Circuits and Systems. 2014;**4**(1):43-56

[45] Möller S, Pommer D, Beyer J, Rake-Revelant J. Factors influencing gaming QoE: Lessons learned from the evaluation of cloud gaming services. In: Proceedings of the 4th International Workshop on Perceptual Quality of Systems (PQS 2013); September 2013: IEEE. 2013. pp. 1-5

[46] Quax P, Beznosyk A, Vanmontfort W, Marx R, Lamotte W. An evaluation of the impact of game genre on user experience in cloud gaming. In: 2013 IEEE International Games Innovation Conference (IGIC); September 2013: IEEE. 2013. pp. 216-221

[47] Wang S, Dey S. Modeling and characterizing user experience in a cloud server based mobile gaming approach. In: 2009 IEEE Global Telecommunications Conference (GLOBECOM 2009); November 2009; IEEE. 2009. pp. 1-7

[48] Wen ZY, Hsiao HF. QoE-driven performance analysis of cloud gaming services. In: 2014 IEEE 16th International Workshop on Multimedia Signal Processing (MMSP); September 2014; IEEE. 2014. pp. 1-6

[49] Chen K-T, Chang Y-C, Hsu H-J, Chen D-Y, Huang C-Y, Hsu C-H. On the quality of service of cloud gaming systems. IEEE Transactions on Multimedia. September 2013;**16**(2):480-495

[50] Huang CY, Hsu CH, Chang YC, Chen KT. Gaming Anywhere: An open cloud gaming system. In: Proceedings of the 4th ACM Multimedia Systems Conference; February 2013; ACM. 2013. pp. 36-47

[51] Manzano M, Uruena M, Sužnjević M, Calle E, Hernandez JA, Matijasevic M. Dissecting the protocol and network traffic of the OnLive cloud gaming platform. Multimedia Systems. 2014;**20**(5):451-470

[52] Cai W, Leung VC, Hu L. A cloudlet-assisted multiplayer cloud gaming system. Mobile Networks and Applications. 2014;**19**(2):144-152

[53] Sun K, Wu D. Video rate control strategies for cloud gaming. Journal of Visual Communication and Image Representation. 2015;**30**:234-241

[54] Liu Y, Dey S, Lu Y. Enhancing video encoding for cloud gaming using rendering information. IEEE Transactions on Circuits and Systems for Video Technology. 2015;**25**(12):1960-1974

[55] Jarvinen S, Laulajainen JP, Sutinen T, Sallinen S. Qos-aware real-time video encoding how to improve the user experience of a gaming-on-demand service. In: 2006 3rd IEEE Consumer Communications and Networking Conference (CCNC 2006); January 2006; IEEE. Vol. 2. 2006. pp. 994-997

[56] Wang S, Dey S. Addressing response time and video quality in remote server based internet mobile gaming. In: 2010 IEEE Wireless Communication and Networking Conference; April 2010; IEEE. pp. 1-6

[57] Cai W, Shea R, Huang CY, Chen KT, Liu J, Leung VC, et al. A Survey on Cloud Gaming: Future of Computer Games. Vol. 4. IEEE Access; 2016. pp. 7605-7620

[58] Vlada R.H. Strategija obrazovanja, znanosti i tehnologije [Internet]. Zagreb: Narodne Novine; 2013. Available from: https://narodne-novine.nn.hr/clanci/sluzbeni/2014_10_124_2364.html

[59] Perrotta C. Gaming horizons deliverable D1. Final Research Report. 2018. p. 8

[60] Federal Communications Commission [Internet]. 2012. Digital

textbook playbook Available from: https://transition.fcc.gov/files/Digital_Textbook_Playbook.pdf

[61] Stewart J, Bleumers L, Van Looy J, Mariën I, All A, Schurmans D, et al. The Potential of Digital Games for Empowerment and Social Inclusion of Groups at Risk of Social and Economic Exclusion: Evidence and Opportunity for Policy. Seville, Spain: Joint Research Centre, European Commission; 2013

[62] IEEE P802.11 Task group AX [Internet] 2019. Available from: http://www.ieee802.org/11/Reports/tgax_update.htm

[63] Slivar I, Sužnjević M, Skorin-Kapov L, Ilić V. Cloud gaming in education: Evaluation of multiple game streams in a shared WLAN. In: 2016 Zooming Innovation in Consumer Electronics International Conference (ZINC); June 2016; IEEE. 2016. pp. 62-65

[64] McDaniel R, Kenny R. Evaluating the relationship between cognitive style and pre-service teachers' preconceived notions about adopting console video games for use in future classrooms. International Journal of Game-Based Learning. 2013, 2013;**3**(2):55-76. DOI: 10.4018/ijgbl.2013040104

[65] Bleumers L, All A, Mariën I, Schurmans D, Van Looy J, Jacobs A, et al. State of Play of Digital Games for Empowerment and Inclusion: A Review of the Literature and Empirical Cases. Luxembourg: European Commission; 2012. DOI: 10.2791/36295

Chapter 6

Digital Games in Primary Education

Dionysios Manesis

Abstract

Digital educational games create a new perspective in learning culture, which go hand in hand with the interests of the pupils. Digital educational games are an innovation in primary education that can enhance children learning and acquiring skills. The integration of digital educational games in the school environment of primary education could effectively contribute to reforming the educational system. Early childhood education and primary education teachers can play a crucial role in supporting children's digital game-based learning (DGBL). Teachers' beliefs about using DGBL are important and often limit their efforts to integrate new technologies into the classroom. Positive views can help teachers embody DGBL in their teaching methods more easily. Thus, without the knowledge of teachers' views and intentions about using DGBL in primary education settings, any potential innovations in this area may lack utility. The scope of this chapter is to investigate the pedagogical dimension of digital educational games as far as the primary education concerns, examine the factors that influence the effectiveness of games in the learning procedure, give valuable information in the designers of digital educational games, and finally examine primary school teachers' beliefs about DGBL, as well as their confidence in integrating digital educational games in the classroom.

Keywords: digital educational games, digital game-based learning, primary education, pupil, primary education teacher

1. Introduction

Despite the fact that digital games consist, for the younger generation, a distinct form of informal information and communication technology (ICT) literacy practice [1], digital game-based learning (DGBL) has evolved into an integral and part of didactical use of ICT, especially in primary education [2]. Nowadays, digital games are a rapidly expanding field, mainly because they are considered as the most popular technology in children's entertainment. At the same time, digital games, when properly designed and utilized in a pedagogically appropriate manner, can be utilized as learning tools to improve the effectiveness of the learning process at all levels of education.

Literature on primary education and DGBL [3–17] has emphasized that digital educational games can enhance children's learning, social interactions, proper behaviors, problem-solving, higher order thinking, critical ability, memory, and eye-hand coordination skills. In addition, in primary education, digital educational games are seen as a dynamic tool for developing pupils' cognitive skills and enhancing their learning motivation. For example, when a pupil completes an activity through an appropriately customized digital educational game, deals better with cognitive concepts, and is able to embrace the key points of a module more easily. Furthermore, pupils often take responsibility for their own learning style and consequently become more autonomous in their actions and decisions [18].

The overall aim of this chapter is to investigate the pedagogical aspects of digital educational games in the primary education. This chapter also aims at examining the factors that influence the effectiveness of games in the learning procedure, giving valuable information in the designers of educational policy as far as the DGBL concerns. Finally, the specific chapter examines primary school teachers' views about DGBL, as well as their confidence in using digital educational games into the classroom. Teachers' views are essential for DGBL integration in primary education settings, as positive views are crucial for influencing their decisions to use DGBL methods in their teaching. It is thus crucial to investigate primary school teachers' views and intentions about integrating and using digital educational games in their classroom. Their views and intentions may predict the integration of DGBL in primary education, while successful integration will also depend on other parameters such as appropriate skills and training. Such an investigation is also helpful for the design of primary school teacher training programs. The content of related modules could take into account teachers' views and intentions and address them accordingly.

2. Definition of digital games

There is a wide range of terms and definitions in literature related to digital games, mainly due to the existence of multiple digital media designed for gaming. As a consequence, the meaning of digital games has become synonymous to a wide range or terms, such as computer games, digital games, electronic games and video games. A brief definition of digital games entails their description as a wide variety of digital applications characterized by some common elements (e.g., the gaming environment, the strong participation of the gamer, the element of interactivity, and an increased use of multimedia) [19].

According to Prensky in [20] (pp. 118–119), a game can be defined as digital based on six characteristics leading to the gamer's involvement (when combined). These are the following characteristics:

- The rules of the game.
- The aims of the game.
- The result and its feedback.
- The element of conflict/competition/challenge/rivalry.
- The element of interaction.
- The representation of a story or plot.

Digital games are based on predetermined rules and limitations which lead the player toward a clear goal also defined by a specific challenge. The features of such games interact constantly with the player, while providing feedback either through scoring or through changes made in the world of the game, thus allowing players constant watch over their progress and practice their skills through overcoming numerous obstacles during gaming [19, 21–23].

3. Definition of digital educational games

Digital educational games are software applications which combine both the characteristics of video games and those of computer-based games. They aim to design enticing learning experiences that successfully correspond to specific learning aims and results [24]. Digital educational games also take into account the desire and enthusiasm of students toward playing, while encouraging the development of logical thinking and the acquisition of knowledge, abilities, and skills. They can potentially stimulate the interest of the most demanding of students by assimilating them into the learning process through activities away from the traditional didactic methods adopted by most schools. In order to achieve this, digital educational games make use of multimedia and Internet technologies. At this point, the student has the ability to comprehend the demanding terms of a learning subject in his own learning pace through interactive and engaging applications and activities. Additionally, the possibility for socialization, cooperation, and creative expression is offered to learners of all grades through their interaction with digital environments and virtual worlds [25].

Digital educational games are considered to be attractive because of their entertaining features in combination with their pleasant environment, their esthetic quality (graphics, effects, music), the existence of a structured framework, their learning goals (also presented as problems demanding solution), and the existence of the gaming dimension (causing also the strong participation of the learner) [26]. As a learning approach, digital educational games are considered to be contemporary learning tools and modern mediums of learning by bringing education to a new dimension. When used appropriately in an organized learning framework (with specific learning objectives, appropriate developmental design, and evaluation), digital educational games can be classified as active learning environments [26].

4. Classification and characteristics of digital educational games

According to their educational use, digital educational games can be classified into three major categories: educational games, leisure games, and educational leisure games [27]. The main definition of educational games refers to games designed with specific educational aims in order to support the teaching and learning processes. This definition includes games belonging to the "serious games" category, to "edutainment," "game-based simulations," and "epistemic games." Leisure games are defined as games which do not promote learning as a clear and exclusive aim, although they also do not exclude their potential use when enforcing learning. This category consists of commercial games, also known as commercial off-the-shelf games (COTS games). Educational leisure games are those used in class or in laboratory to support and enforce teaching and learning despite the fact these are designed for commercial purposes (e.g., The Sims, RollerCoaster Tycoon series, Civilization, and Age of Empires). This category is also continuously being expanded since digital gaming market companies are aware of the possible future inclusion of digital games in education, in universities, and even in military training.

Digital educational games do not set enjoyment and fun as their primary objective, but their environment includes educational content in a challenging and enjoyable way which promotes active learning [22]. From a bird's-eye view, digital educational games must harmonize engagement, challenge, entertainment, and learning [28]. Digital educational games are based on four main elements which are engagement, autonomy, mastery, and progression. Engagement is connecting the player with the educational content of the game. Digital educational games allow player to be more autonomous as far as the ability to make decisions and take appropriate action is concerned. Mastery is the degree of repeatability of players' specific actions in order to gain full control of the game. Progression refers to the reward to players for their success. In fact, progression is the main motivation for players to accomplish the game's goals while learning at the same time [29]. The evaluation of digital educational games can be conducted through several quality characteristics: game design, user interface, engagement, enjoyment, usability, playability, usefulness, cognitive behavior, pedagogical aspects, and learning outcomes [22].

5. The use of digital educational games in primary education

The didactic model of traditional teaching can be deemed as a noneffective method, which cannot also ensure great learning outcomes (at least as demanded by contemporary society). The current generation of pupils seems to lack motivation and satisfactory learning results as encountered in the existing traditional educational system [30]. Bodies from all educational levels need to redesign their schedules as well as their policies on the use and incorporation of DGBL corresponding thus to the current digital literacy level of learners. In addition, digital educational games are suitable for digital natives [31]. Indeed, this is one of the main reasons behind the increased levels of use of digital educational games in primary schools.

Educational games offer a new perspective toward the culture of learning, which conforms to the habits and interests of learners. According to a relevant report by the Federation of American Scientists, the integration and use of digital educational games in the school environment could effectively contribute to the reformation of the educational system [32]. When adding the element of entertainment in the learning process, education becomes not only more interesting and pleasant but also more effective [33]. As a result, digital educational games can successfully promote pupil participation, cooperation, and the development of problem-solving strategies [34]. Digital educational games can also place the learner-player into a situation described best by the term "flow" which is characterized by an increased attention span where all demanding tasks seem to be simple and fun. Learners are encouraged to learn by playing digital educational games, since such games offer an alternative learning environment which is both fun and effective.

All appropriate digital educational games can be very useful and effective educational tools, providing an alternative way of presenting educational content [35]. The educational organization known as *Common Sense Media* supports the belief that appropriately designed educational games do not distract pupils. On the contrary, they can be used as support channels for all practices and types of learning and teaching. Additionally, digital educational games can motivate students independent of gender, age, or level of education, while offering an appropriate environment to different learning groups, for achieving common learning goals through cooperation. Educational games may also support teachers in their attempt to teach different types of pupils [36, 37].

As Klopfer et al. described in [38], digital educational games are usually defined as rich and exciting learning environments because they allow players to access environments otherwise impossible (e.g., players can go back to the story, manage entire civilizations, or handle the intricate operation of a big city). Digital educational games that include virtual worlds and simulations can also be transformed into necessary educational tools, mainly due to promoting and upgrading participatory interactive and entertaining activities [39]. All appropriately designed games are able to support learners in developing such abilities and skills that will be proven valuable to the real world and which cannot be effectively taught through traditional teaching [40]. This fact could be applied to primary school students. Such an example could be "The Sims" game addressing students of all ages, while assisting in the simulation of social situations through a variety of unpredictable situations (e.g., the role of economic goods and the relations between family members). Another example could be the game titled "Minecraft" whose sales exceed those of 20 million copies.

Primary education is considered to be the most appropriate of all levels of education for the integration of digital educational games to occur. This happens due to the fact that primary schools can adequately respond to new and complex development-related challenges. In primary education, there is need for profound change, while the use of DGBL can be easily implemented through expanding and supporting the existing traditional teaching methods. The following components support the assumption of an efficient integration of digital educational games in primary education through:

- A framework for the introduction of ICT in primary education teaching and learning called "Cross-Thematic Curriculum Framework for ICT." This framework mentions ICT as an essential part of education and a powerful tool for both pupils and teachers. It is also important for children to always come in systematic contact with technology for their all-rounded development.
- The flexibility of the curriculum.
- The combination of digital educational games with the curriculum in an easy and immediate manner.
- The prospects for the evolution of digital educational games based on the relatively positive views of the majority of primary school teachers (especially of the young ones).
- The pupils' psychological and emotional development through the use of digital educational games.

Furthermore, DGBL can enhance the study program of primary education as far as the ways of promoting learning are concerned. The educational system can make use of the energy and passion displayed by pupils on digital educational games in order to use these for improving its learning processes, based on the acquisition of meaningful abilities and skills. The incorporation of new technologies in the game is indeed essential to the learning process in all stages of development.

According to Shaffer in [40], there are certain principles which explain the way of learning through the use of digital educational games:

- All previously acquired knowledge by the learner is in position to both assist and hinder learning. Undoubtedly, all pre-existing knowledge upon a subject is favorable. If someone's knowledge is flawed, this will become obvious only through a test when sticking to the traditional learning method. In the case of learning through digital educational games, the same person will be able to trace his problematic point easily and fast, since one wrong move leads to consequences. By doing this, the user will be able to correct himself and move forward.

- The learners' motives direct, define, and support their steps toward learning. Learners are usually motivated by scores and the progress of games. For example, they play persistently until they reach a safe score in the game. Through this process, they learn how to act in the environment of the game, how to experiment, and how to think and learn about the completion of a task. In this way, they develop a productive and consistent way of thinking.

- Learners need to acquire abilities and skills for perfecting and applying all knowledge acquired. Usually, the design of a game is focused on rules and learning parameters without dwelling on their possible application. In contrast, all well-designed games are adjusted to each player and his learning pace. The learner keeps his basic knowledge as a starting point, but he cannot move forward without completing all levels. So, the game represents a realistic, interactive, and active learning environment that is focused on thinking, learning, and applying the appropriate knowledge at the appropriate time.

- Target-based practice is connected to feedback and to the enhancement of quality learning. Traditional learning does not provide any success-motivated feedback and does not offer pupils the possibility of constantly placing their thoughts and abilities in a realistic environment. In digital educational games, players are motivated by the aims of the game, while learning through errors and their consequences. Indeed, feedback motivates players to keep trying until they reach the goals of the game, providing them also with all necessary information to succeed.

Users consider games a relaxing and natural activity which leads them to also view computers as gaming tools. At the same time, users expect recognition of their efforts by the game either through feedback or by being encouraged to proceed to more difficult procedures [41]. Through this process, the "I act to learn" model is being developed as opposed to the "I learn before I act" one. Learners also develop their fantasy through the environment of the game, while creating all appropriate conditions to approach new technologies in a friendly way [40].

When considering the use of digital educational games as pedagogical tools, teachers can play an important role by ensuring that their pupils re-evaluate all problems appropriately during the learning activity of the game. Digital educational games can also provide the learner with satisfactory interaction and can offer multiple chances for learning by doing.

Teachers today have to ensure that learners have the appropriate reflexes to gaining knowledge through playing digital educational games. DGBL is considered to be the fundamental component of teaching, although they do not have to play a central role to be deemed as necessary to learners. For example, (see [31]) pupils may be taught a foreign language by the traditional teaching method while in class and practice the language at home using the equivalent digital game. Digital educational games may also have additional value as supplementary teaching/learning material and as source teaching/learning material at the same time.

As new multipurpose mediums that activate pupils' interest and learning, digital educational games offer new perspectives that need to be treated maturely by teachers interested to renew their means of teaching. But it is impossible for digital educational games to be treated as educational materials without fulfilling specific requirements to support in-class learning. Those requirements are a combination of the digital educational games' content and the basic principles of class management, which are fundamental for the development of digital educational games.

Most researches based on the use of DGBL in primary education focus on the investigation of how digital educational games and gamification (the strategic use of games' elements to reach a goal) can be used to motivate students, to improve their skills, and to maximize their knowledge in different disciplines [3, 42–44].

6. Effectiveness of digital educational games as learning tools

A part of the research conducted is based on digital educational games and their ability to pique the interest of students. This investigation indicates that most digital educational games display some common characteristics such as the sense of control, curiosity, and the cases of intrinsic and extrinsic fantasy [26]. Based on such results, some teachers seem to support the use of digital educational games as part of didactic activities. Digital educational games are those types of games which encourage the development of logical thinking and the acquisition of knowledge and skills in a pleasant manner. Their background is connected to pieces of knowledge that users need to apply in order to achieve all goals proposed. The additional value brought to the educational aspect of digital educational games is based on the motives introduced to learners supporting the gain of knowledge while having fun. At the same time, the use of multimedia and all interesting stories can become "partners" of the user during the game leading to the achievement of all learning goals [26, 41].

On the other hand, there are many factors which can influence the effectiveness of digital educational games. These factors are related to the user's personal traits, his preferences, and personality, since not everyone has the same style and attitude while interacting with digital educational games or during problem-solving. For that matter, designers of digital educational games make use of various teaching methods and strategies for developing their digital game environment. One of the most important processes for the creation of acceptable and motivating activities is the technique of placing the user's abilities and the challenges encountered within acceptable limits. By doing this, the user will not be left with feelings of boredom, lack of fun, worry, or stress. When the challenge is above the user's abilities, it usually brings up feelings of anguish and disappointment, while a challenge below the user's abilities will probably bring a sense of monotony [45].

It must be mentioned that there are several uncertainties, concerning the learning effectiveness of digital educational games. For example, there is gap of consensus concerning the factors that may have an impact on DGBL effectiveness. As a result, more sophisticated assessment models are needed, which will take into account more direct or indirect factors and interactions [46].

During the past years, the spread of digital educational games has instigated further research on their potential as learning tools (especially when addressing younger audiences). The game's environment is considered as impressive and typically captures the attention of users, while the quality of graphics and its realism increases the player's involvement and identification with the game's characters. The user's active role, the challenge presented, his curiosity, the fantasy, and the conflicts are all factors that make players get acquainted with the way the plot of the game is structured and also allow them to engage in the game. The experience of the game is the cause of the player's intrinsic motivation to remember, understand, and apply in accordance with the version of the game's taxonomy of educational objectives [47].

In addition to this, digital educational games allow for an overall presentation of a subject and promote the active role of the user who takes initiatives. They also support stand-alone activities where the activity itself becomes the motive of involvement while the game and the adjustment of its functions occur according to the preferences and level of the user [30]. At the same time, digital educational games can contribute to the achievement of specific learning goals, such as promotion of knowledge, cognitive development, social interaction, and the shaping of attitudes [10]. Digital educational games are effective when increasing the students' skills, in cases such as socialization, cooperation, problem-solving (use of memory and mathematical skills), and the visuomotor coordination [3, 9, 48, 49]. Digital educational games may also provide models of appropriate learning practices [13].

The structure of digital educational games which usually attracts players involves the immediate reaction from the game's environment to each action of the player, its dynamic images, the interaction, the existence of a specific goal, the set of rules, the challenge, and the elements of fantasy and curiosity [29]. Prensky in [26] presents an extensive research on the field of DGBL and the qualities corresponding to different types of learning. All interactive learning techniques applied to digital educational games (e.g., practice and feedback, learning by doing, goal-oriented learning, discovery learning, role-playing, and constructivist learning) render them applicable to a wide range of learning types. All of the features mentioned earlier puff the potential of integrating DGBL into existing educational platforms.

7. The role of the teacher

Despite the fact digital educational games demonstrate great potential of evolving and becoming integrated in primary teaching and learning, their application demands attention in order to exclude all possible weak points from their proper function. The use of digital educational games in a class of primary school demands the teacher's attention on the content, structure, and design parameters. At this point, the teacher plays an important role in order to ensure the quality of learning and the participation of learners. Apart from it being essential, the teacher's role entails also creativity since he is expected to include game-based learning in his teaching techniques. This occurs due to the fact that all primary school curricula do not contain detailed instructions for the appropriate use of digital educational games [2]. So, the teacher is called to integrate games appropriately in his teaching methods, while combining games with a discussion process and extra activities, without the use of the computer since the game by itself might cause confusion to its users [40]. DGBL should also be combined with other educational medium in order to ensure the generalization of knowledge and its application in other fields [34].

When using digital educational games in primary education, the role of the teacher is shared by both computer and learners while each supports a different function [30]:

Computer as teacher	Learners as teachers
It creates a learning environment based on the game's rules of conduct	Learners correct their own mistakes
It changes and adapts according to the level of the user	They advise their classmates on how to achieve goals
It is available at any time and for as much time as needed by the learner	They cooperate with their classmates to find solutions to problems
It may contain appropriate instructions or it can assist in the process of problem-solving	They gain knowledge and dominance over the subject they learn about

Computer as teacher	Learners as teachers
It gives immediate feedback through the results of the learner's actions	
It incorporates learners into a competitive environment while motivating them to become involved	

8. Barriers in the use of DGBL in education

Despite all possible gains deriving from digital educational games, there are many barriers to their inclusion in primary education. Some teachers believe that new technologies are not capable of guaranteeing effective learning on their own, while there is still need for adequate educational designing based on the fundamental principles of learning. As consequence, there is a percentage of teachers remaining skeptical on the use of digital educational games as teaching and learning tools. When introducing a game in class without having a specific educational framework beforehand, it may lead to negative results rather than positive ones, since not all games are appropriate or designed for all types of learners [31]. Because of this, the attention of learners might be diverted from the class, resulting to the failure of the desired learning goals. Then, learners might be unable to get knowledge out of the game, especially when the game is based on a wrongly designed environment of contact or when it is structured on elusive learning goals. Other researchers participating in the creation and designing of games are worried that games based on facilitating learning might result in losing their appeal to learners [37].

The simple use of DGBL in education seems to be insufficient as there is much more need for their correct use, combined with effective systems of learning. For example, games are not deemed as appropriate in education on the basis of their 3D graphics but on their application inside and outside of the primary education classroom. The main goal of a typical DGBL activity is to result in a combination of knowledge and entertainment. This is not always feasible, though, as there are certain elements reproduced in successful games whose incorporation does not necessarily guarantee a great educational outcome [2, 48].

Literature refers to two types of barriers encountered by teachers that might place limitations to the successful application of digital educational games in teaching. Firstly, there are external barriers like the lack of time, lack of education, limited funding, and limited access. It is rather difficult for teachers to incorporate digital educational games during a single teaching hour, especially when there is lack of time, support, and access to media. Teachers also lack further training on how to use digital educational games effectively in class. For that matter, the lack of time, lack of motives, and lack of support discourage teachers from becoming involved with DGBL [2].

Secondly, there are internal barriers for the exclusion of computer games from classroom, such as teacher's personal beliefs (e.g., his negative attitudes toward digital educational games), his lack of interest, and his lack of confidence in using digital educational games as didactic tools [2]. This hesitation based on the appropriateness of digital educational games according to age and content might be subdued by the possibility of selecting age-appropriate computer games from the age rating system of Pan European Game Information (PEGI). The PEGI system takes into consideration the appropriateness of a game according to age—not according to level of difficulty or the user's abilities. This system includes age rating labels and other types of labels based on content, which can ultimately guide parents and teachers when choosing the age-appropriate digital game [49].

9. Conclusion

With the increased popularity of ICT, the use of digital educational games to support learning has recently gained new meaning [48]. The incorporation of digital educational games in primary education in order to teach multiple terms is indeed necessary, as even those involved in the process recognize the importance of the digital educational games as assistive learning tools. The majority of research conducted on the basis of the use of digital educational games confirms the positive relation between learning and engaging pupils with digital educational games, while motivating them to acquire or check their knowledge in a pleasant and creative manner. Although there are many difficulties in the integration of digital educational games in the class, the use of digital educational games, as a breakthrough teaching and learning tool, has great growth prospects.

The ministry of education, the designers of educational policies and curricula, the administration of primary education, and teachers on their own have to support the integration and use of digital educational games in teaching and learning processes. The training of teachers on the value of digital educational games is also of great importance. Teachers' confidence in digital educational games can be enhanced by attending properly designed training programs that will provide teachers with the appropriate skills in order to evaluate and implement appropriate DGBL in primary education. In parallel, there is need for technical, financial, and administrative support.

The conduct of further research is necessary for exploring all factors and parameters in the use and integration of digital educational games in primary education. There are also suggestions for designing and creating appropriate digital educational games, using contemporary scenarios, and being compatible with the expected learning outcomes. This will eventually allow the active participation of all users-learners and the creation of digital learning communities, which will render learning a more pleasant and engaging process.

Author details

Dionysios Manesis
National and Kapodistrian University of Athens, Athens, Greece

*Address all correspondence to: manesis_d@yahoo.com

References

[1] Kankaanrata M, Koivula M, Laakso ML, Mustola M. Digital games in early childhood: Broadening definitions of learning, literacy, and play, serious games and edutainment applications. Springer Link. 2017;**2**:349-367. DOI: 10.1080/09669760.2013.772049

[2] Manesis D. Obstacles to games-based learning in early childhood education: Cyprus teachers' perceptions. In: Proceedings of the 17th European Conference on e-Learning; 1-2 November 2018. Greece. ISBN: 978-1-912764-07-5. pp. 361-369

[3] Allsop Y, Yeniman Yildirim E, Screpanti M. Teachers' beliefs about game based learning: A comparative study of pedagogy, curriculum and practice in Italy, Turkey and the UK. In: Proceedings of the 7th European Conference on Games-Based Learning; 3-4 October 2013. Vol. 1. Portugal. ISBN: 978-1-909507-65-4. pp. 1-10

[4] Kokkalia G, Economou A, Roussos P, Choli S. The use of serious games in preschool education. International Journal of Emerging Technologies in Learning (iJET). 2017;**12**(11):15-27. DOI: 10.3991/ijet.v12.i11.6991

[5] Divjak B, Tomic D. The impact of game-based learning on the achievement of learning goals and motivation for learning mathematics - literature review. Journal of Information and Organizational Sciences. 2011;**1**(1):15-30. DOI: 10.31341/jios

[6] Doliopoulou E, Rizou C. Greek kindergarten teachers' and parents' views about changes in play since their own childhood. European Early Childhood Education Research Journal. 2012;**20**(1):133-147. DOI: 10.1080/1350293X.2012.650016

[7] Edwards S. Digital play in the early years: A contextual response to the problem of integrating technologies and play-based pedagogies in the early childhood curriculum. European Early Childhood Education Research Journal. 2013;**21**(2):199-212. DOI: 10.1080/1350293X.2013.789190

[8] Fessakis G, Gouli E, Mavroudi E. Problem solving by 5-6 years old kindergarten children in a computer programming environment: A case study. Computers in Education. 2013;**63**:87-97. DOI: 10.1016/j.compedu.2012.11.016

[9] Koivisto A, Kiili K, Perttula A. Designing educational exertion games for young children. In: Proceedings of the 5th European Conference on Games-Based Learning; 20-21 October 2011. Greece. ISBN: 978-1-908272-18-8-Book. pp. 322-328

[10] Lieberman DA, Chesley Fisk M, Biely E. Digital games for young children ages three to six: From research to design. Computers in the Schools. 2009;**26**(4):299-313. DOI: 10.1080/07380560903360178

[11] Ezziyyani M. Early childhood education: How play can be used to meet children's individual needs. In: Advanced Intelligent Systems for Sustainable Development (AI2SD'2018). Switzerland: Springer Nature; 2019. pp. 232-245. DOI: 10.1007/978-3-030-11884-6_22

[12] Manessis D. Early childhood post-educated teachers' views and intentions about using digital games in the classroom. In: Proceedings of the 5th European Conference on Games-Based Learning; 20-21 October 2011. Greece. ISBN: 978-1-908272-18-8-Book. pp. 753-758

[13] Manessis D. Examining early childhood education students' attitudes toward educational computer games in

kindergarten. In: Proceedings of the 7th European Conference on Games-Based Learning; 3-4 October 2013. Vol. 1. Portugal. ISBN: 978-1-909507-65-4. pp. 369-377

[14] Stephen C, Plowman L. Digital Play. In: Brooker L, Blaise M, Edwards S, editors. SAGE Handbook of Play and Learning in Early Childhood. London: SAGE; 2014. pp. 1-15. DOI: 10.4135/9781473907850.n28

[15] Verenikina I, Herrington R, Peterson R, Mantei J. Computers and play in early childhood: Affordances and limitations. Journal of Interactive Learning Research. 2010;**21**(1):139-159 ISSN 1093-023X

[16] Yien JM, Hung CM, Hwang GJ, Lin YCA. Game-based learning approach to improving students' learning achievements in a nutrition course. The Turkish Online Journal of Educational Technology. 2011;**10**(2):1-10

[17] Zevenbergen R, Logan H. Computer use by preschool children: Rethinking practice as digital natives come to preschool. Australasian Journal of Early Childhood. 2008;**33**(1):37-44. DOI: 10.1177/183693910803300107

[18] Sumuer E, Yakin I. Effects of an educational game development course on preservice teachers' concerns about the use of computer games in the classroom. In: Proceedings of the 9th International Educational Technology Conference (IETC2009); 6-8 May 2009. Turkey; 2009

[19] Carr D, Buckingham D, Burn A, Scott G. Computer Games: Text, Narrative and Play. Wiley: Polity Press; 2006. 224 p. ISBN: 978-0-745-63400-5

[20] Prensky M. Digital Game-Based Learning. New York, NY: McGraw-Hill; 2001. 431 p

[21] Zhonggen Y. A meta-analysis of use of serious games in education over a decade. International Journal of Computer Games Technology. 2019;**2019**:1-8. DOI: 10.1155/2019/4797032

[22] Abdellatif A, McCollum B, McMullan P. Serious games: Quality characteristics evaluation framework and case study. In: Proceedings of the Integrated STEM Education Conference (ISEC); 10 March 2018. USA. DOI: 10.1109/ISECon.2018.8340460

[23] Vogel JJ, Vogel DS, Cannon-Bowers J, Bowers CA, Muse K, Wright M. Computer gaming and interactive simulations for learning: A meta-analysis. Journal of Educational Computing Research. 2006;**34**:229-243. DOI: 10.2190/FLHV-K4WA-WPVQ-H0YM

[24] de Freitas S. Learning in Immersive Worlds. Bristol: Joint Information Systems Committee; 2007. p. 73

[25] Malliet S. An exploration of adolescents' perceptions of videogame realism. Learning, Media and Technology. 2006;**31**:377-394. DOI: 10.1080/17439880601021983

[26] Prensky M. Digital Game-Based Learning. St. Paul, MN: Paragon House Publishers; 2007. 464 p

[27] Ulicsak M, Williamson B. Computer games and learning; Futurelab. 2010. Available from: https://www.nfer.ac.uk/media/1765/futl01.pdf

[28] Kaimara P, Deliyannis I. Why should I play this game? The role of motivation in smart pedagogy. In: Daniela L, editor. Didactics of Smart Pedagogy (113-137). Cham: Springer; 2019. DOI: 10.1007/978-3-030-01551-0_6

[29] Pitarch RC. An approach to digital game-based learning: Video-games

principles and applications in foreign language learning. Journal of Language Teaching and Research. 2018;**9**(6):1147-1159. DOI: /10.17507/jltr.0906.04

[30] Gee JP. What Video Games Have to Teach us about Learning and Literacy. New York: Palgrave Macmillan; 2003. 256p. ISBN-10: 1403961697

[31] Ince EY. Educational Games in Higher Education, Simulation and Gaming, Dragan Cvetković. London: InTechOpen; 2017. DOI: 10.5772/intechopen.71017

[32] Kebritchia M, Hirumi A, Bai H. The effects of modern mathematics computer games on mathematics achievement and class motivation. Computers in Education. 2010;**55**:427-443. DOI: 10.1016/j.compedu.2010.02.007

[33] Prensky M. The motivation of gameplay. On the Horizon. 2002;**10**(1): 5-11. DOI: 10.1108/10748120210431349

[34] Gros B. Digital games in education: The Design of Games-Based Learning Environments. Journal of Research on Technology in Education. 2007;**40**(1):23-28. DOI: 10.1080/15391523.2007.10782494

[35] Protopsaltis A, Pannese L, Pappa D, Hetzner S. Serious games and formal and informal learning. eLearning Papers. 2011;**25**:1-10

[36] Allen G, Sosnik E, Swanson K, White C. Achievement unlocked digital games as a key for learning. In: A Whitepaper for K-12 Parents, Guardians, Family Members. San Francisco: BrightBytes Labs & co.lab; 2013

[37] Papadakis S. The use of computer games in classroom environment. International Journal of Teaching and Case Studies. 2018;**9**(1):1-25. DOI: 10.1504/IJTCS.2018.10011113

[38] Klopfer E, Scheintaub H, Huang W, Roque WD. R. (2009). The simulation cycle - combining games, simulations, engineering and science using StarLogo TNG. Journal of E-Learning and Digital Media. 2009;**6**(1):71-96. DOI: 10.2304/elea.2009.6.1.71

[39] Thomas K. A social worker took the kids away: The power of games to help children learn; Futurelab publications. 2009. Available from: http://archive.futurelab.org.uk/resources/publications-reports-articles/web-articles/Web-Article1507

[40] Shaffer DW. How Computer Games Help Children Learn. 2006th ed. New York: Amazon; 2006. p. 242. DOI: 10.1057/9780230601994

[41] Ke F. A case study of computer gaming for math: Engaged learning from gameplay? Computers in Education. 2008;**51**(4):1609-1620. DOI: 10.1016/j.compedu.2008.03.003

[42] Jones BA, Madden GJ, Wengreen HJ, Aguilar SS, Desjardins EA. Gamification of dietary decision-making in an elementary-school cafeteria. PLoS One. 2014;**9**(4):e93872. DOI: 10.1371/journal.pone.0093872

[43] Kickmeier-Rust MD, Hillemann EC, Albert D. Gamification and smart feedback: Experiences with a primary school level math app. International Journal of Game-Based Learning (IJGBL). 2014;**4**(3):35-46. DOI: 10.4018/ijgbl.2014070104

[44] Gooch D, Vasalou A, Benton L, Khaled R. Using gamification to motivate students with dyslexia. In: Proceedings of the 2016 CHI Conference on Human Factors in Computing Systems; 07-12 May 2016. USA. pp. 969-980. DOI: 10.1145/2858036.2858231

[45] Dondlinger MJ. Educational video game design: A review of the literature.

Journal of Applied Educational Technology. 2007;**4**(1):21-31

[46] Fokides E, Atsikpasi P, Kaimara P, Deliyannis I. Factors influencing the subjective learning effectiveness of serious games. Journal of Information Technology Education: Research. 2019;**18**:437-466. DOI: 10.28945/4441

[47] Calderon A, Ruiz M. A systematic literature review on serious games evaluation: An application to software project management. Computers in Education. 2015;**87**:396-422. DOI: 10.1016/j.compedu.2015.07.011

[48] Manessis D. The importance of future kindergarten teachers' beliefs about the usefulness of games based. International journal of games-based. Learning. 2014;**4**(1):78-90. DOI: 10.4018/IJGBL.2014010105

[49] Felicia P. Digital Games in Schools: A Handbook for Teachers. Brussels, Belgium: European Schoolnet; 2009. 47p. Hal-00697599

Chapter 7

World of Warcraft Stats System: Evolution and Casualization

Adrián Domínguez, Daniel Vallés-Blanco, Luis de-Marcos, Juan Aguado-Delgado and Sergio Caro-Alvaro

Abstract

Since World of Warcraft release, it has remained as the MMORPG with more subscribers of the market, and during that time, it has evolved in diverse ways. One of the aspects that have suffered more changes is its character stats system, which is an elemental part of this game. By studying it, we can learn much about the game evolution. Some players feel that the game has evolved to appeal to more casual audiences. In this study, we will analyze the development of World of Warcraft character stats system through the expansions while trying to determine if these changes have promoted the casualization of the game. Study results could be interesting for game designers and game researchers as an example of the long-term evolution of one of the most important computer games in history.

Keywords: MMORPG, casual, game design, game studies, game industry

1. Introduction

MMORPG stands for massively multiplayer online role-playing games. Two different terms form this name, MMO and RPG. MMOs are online games that bring together many players in the same persistent world. The world is still active when the player disconnects and continues advancing without him until he reconnects. RPGs are games in which players are allowed to share the creation of their own story, where they play a main character [1]. A digital RPG is a role-playing game very similar to board role-playing games. According to Thomas H. Apparely, " ... the key difference between paper and pencil RPGs and computer RPGs is that the game is no longer a collectively produced fantasy, but one that takes place in an official fantasy world with strict parameters defined" [2]. Therefore, an MMORPG is an RPG game in which a large number of players participate online in the same persistent world and interact with each other to achieve a common goal.

World of Warcraft, the title that we will analyze in this work, is precisely one of the most influential and relevant MMORPGs in history [3]. It was released on November 23, 2004, in North America, and on February 11, 2005, in Europe. Since then, Blizzard has been taking expansions of the game every few years, in addition to constant updates for each expansion. These changes have affected every aspect of the game, making World of Warcraft one of the games that has suffered more evolution along time.

Many players consider that World of Warcraft evolution has gravitated towards a more easy to play game, removing complex aspects that required an in-depth knowledge of the game mechanics to perform optimally, thus making the game more casual. Casualization is a phenomenon related to the game design, which consists in making various changes to the mechanics, difficulty, and effort required to facilitate mastering the game. Traditionally, MMORPGs required players to play for long times to progress in the game, and World of Warcraft, at least in its origins, was no exception.

One of the parts of the game in which fans consider that the casualization process had more impact is in the character stats. In World of Warcraft, each player takes control of a character or avatar through which he interacts with the game world. The characters are characterized, among other aspects, by their stats. According to Salen and Zimmerman, stats, also known as attributes, represent "qualities of objects that are part of a system" [4]. In this case, stats are qualities of characters that are part of the different game systems, such as craft, trade, or combat systems. Among these, the stats related to the combat system are probably the most important, as combat has been one of the main and more complex mechanics of interaction with the environment in World of Warcraft and many other commercial MMORPGs.

Character stats related to the combat system represent qualities such as their strength, agility, or resistance when fighting against other characters. A stat "is formed by an identifier and a value" [5]. The identifier indicates which character quality represents that attribute, while the value indicates the magnitude of the quality. The value of a stat depends on each game. For example, in "Dungeons & Dragons," it is usually between 1 and 20, 10 being the average value of a human being, 20 being a value only attainable by gods and 1 representing the practical lack of that quality. In contrast, in World of Warcraft, the attributes may have values above 300 without being considered high, and, in fact, the scale of stats values has undergone numerous changes throughout the life of the game.

In this work, we will study the evolution of World of Warcraft combat stats system along the successive expansions that have taken place since the title's launch. Our interest is to understand the reasons and motives behind the successive changes it has suffered and to determine if it has been casualized over time, as many players suggest, and, in that case, what are the changes that have been made by designers to simplify the game making it more casual?

2. Study design

Over the years, World of Warcraft has remained as the subscription-based MMORPG with more players all around the world, even entering the *Guinness World Records* as "The most popular MMORPG in number of subscribers with 10 million players in January 2008" [6]. Since then, the game has undergone numerous updates to maintain this success. One of the aspects of the game most affected by the updates, as we can see later, has been the character stats system.

According to some authors, the game has been casualized over the years. In its first versions, the need to exchange information, coordinate with other players, and receive help, encouraged interaction and socialization, but as a result of casualization, cooperation becomes obsolete, and socialization is no longer necessary [7]. Other authors suggest, on the contrary, that casualization was essential for the commercial success of the game in the long term [8]. In any case, despite the various opinions about the World of Warcraft casualization, we have not found papers that analyze how it occurred at the playable level.

2.1 Objective

In this work, we will study in detail the evolution of character stats system and their effect on the World of Warcraft combat system since its launch, to understand how the design of such an important game has evolved and to analyze whether and how the effects of these changes have contributed to its casualization.

This general objective can be summarized in the following research questions:

- Has World of Warcraft suffered a casualization process since its launch due to the changes in its stats system?

    1. Have been character stats required to play optimally reduced?

    2. Has been the improvement of character stats facilitated?

    3. Have been the game mechanics related to stats simplified?

2.2 Methodology

In the first place, we have recovered and synthesized information about World of Warcraft stats system and its evolution throughout the successive expansions, from the first version of the game, commonly called Vanilla, to the Legion expansion that was launched on August 14, 2018. To do so, we have processed the changelogs of these expansions and of other game updates that happened between them. This information has been later analyzed both quantitatively and qualitatively to determine their relation to game casualization.

To answer research question 1.1, we have driven a quantitative analysis comparing the stats available in each expansion. We have divided stats into four groups, one for each role that a character can take in combat: attack, defense, offensive spells, and healing spells. For each role we have identified the stats that a player would require to consider to play optimally. We have compared the amount and variety of these stats through expansions. This comparison allows us to determine the effort and complexity of decisions needed to equip a character optimally for his role. It also gives us insights on the necessary adaptations that a player must perform to play different roles.

Regarding question 1.2, we have separated each expansion stats in two groups, "item stats" that include those which can be directly improved by equipping items and "non-item stats" that include those which are derived from other "item stats" or that are obtained by other game mechanics, such as talents or abilities. We made this distinction because "item stats" are those that require more effort and planning to be increased, as a player can only get the best items by beating end-game quests and enemies. On the contrary, a player can obtain "non-item stats" by increasing the associated "item stats" or by activating talents or abilities, which are unlocked by leveling up. A reduction of "item stats" in favor of "non-item stats" would probably mean that the improvement of stats has been facilitated by making them depend on the character level and not on the acquisition of items, which require much more effort.

Finally, for question 1.3, we have performed a qualitative analysis on every change that the stats system and the related game mechanics have suffered through expansions, to determine if there has been a progressive simplification of game mechanics over time, requiring less effort or knowledge from the players to play optimally.

2.3 Scope

The scope of the study is limited to the evolution of the character's stats related to the combat system in the context of "player vs. environment" game mode, excluding "player vs. player" stats, as well as any other stats that may be related to non-combat game systems such as movement, professions, trading, etc.

The scope will also be limited to changes that affect stat types and their related game mechanics, but we have ignored changes that affect stats values, due solely to the balancing of the game. We will also exclude changes in other game-design aspects, like items or professions, only mentioning them when related to a change that affect character stats types and their associated game mechanics.

3. State of the art

3.1 Studies about World of Warcraft

World of Warcraft, due to its great importance in the field of video games, has been analyzed extensively from various points of view, such as sociological, anthropological, educational, mathematical, and ludological. Several of these studies also mention issues related to the casualization of the game. Below we discuss some of them, highlighting the aspects associated with this work.

In the article "Communication, Coordination, and Camaraderie in World of Warcraft," the author talks about the relationships and communication between players that occurs in a band group [9]. The article explains how they manage to win, despite not having the necessary equipment, thanks to teamwork, the excellent atmosphere of the group, and the coordination between them. Even when focused on communication, the article talks about the combat system and the character stats when it explains how, as soon as the band starts, players talk about how much fire resistance they have. According to the author, players need 180 fire resistances to overcome the mission. Despite players not reaching those values, they continue playing with a friendly and positive mood.

Another sociological cutting study would be "Analyzing the Evolution of Social Groups in World of Warcraft" [8]. This article discusses 192 million data, out of 18 million characters, from 1.4 million teams, over 4 years to investigate World of Warcraft's guilds and their evolution over time. The study differentiates eight different archetypes of guilds based on their activity level throughout the Vanilla game and the first two expansions. Regarding the casual play, the findings say that they have found a strong tendency towards brotherhoods aimed at the casual player. They also argue: "For the design of future games, our conclusion at this point is that for commercial success, it is of major importance to cater to the needs of the casual gamer."

Following this line, we can find articles like "Hardcore Gamers and Casual Gamers Playing Online Together" [10], which talks about how it is necessary to adapt MMO games to casual audiences, since they are quite expensive games to make and maintain that need to reach a broad audience. In the conclusions, they state: "To retain hardcore players, their time and dedication should continue to be rewarded, but should not be the main criterion in order to reduce the frustration of casual players." They also explain how World of Warcraft has shown improvements in this aspect in relation to previous MMORPGs.

We can also find articles that talk about World of Warcraft in more specific aspects of gameplay, such as "Optimizing Play: How Theorycraft Changes Gameplay and Design" [11], which explains how players can influence the design of

DOI: http://dx.doi.org/10.5772/intechopen.90533

the game, and in particular the combat and stats systems, through the theorycraft. The theorycraft consists in analyzing the game mathematically to find a way to maximize the power of the characters, statistically speaking. This way, players can understand what items are more powerful, which spell settings or abilities will be most suitable for them, etc. This practice affects the guilds, who expect to perform well, and also designers, who must balance the game content and design by considering that players will use the theorycraft to optimize their actions.

Concerning the design of video games, we can find "GDC: Learning from World of Warcraft's Quest Design mistakes" [12], which collects a GDC talk by Jeff Kaplan, the then-creative director of World of Warcraft. This talk discusses World of Warcraft missions, their function, and lessons learned from mistakes made when designing them. It explains design problems such as giving too many options to players, thus losing control over the user experience, or writing very long texts or uninteresting missions that are not read, among many other problems and proposals to solve them.

We can also find articles that demonstrate the importance of World of Warcraft in the video game industry. In "The Warning of the World of Warcraft Effect" [12], the author tells us what he calls "wow effect," a tendency of videogame industry to create new MMOs in an attempt to take a share of the market that emerged from the success of World of Warcraft. The author explains that this effect is not unique and resurfaces every time a game becomes the norm, setting as an example "Minecraft," "Call of Duty," or "Fortnite," among others. It suggests that developers should avoid falling for this effect, as it is challenging to compete against a game that has been on the market longer and leads the genre in question.

3.2 Studies about casual games

Focusing on the field of casual play, an essential point of this work, we can also find several relevant studies that specifically address this topic. An important aspect is to know what "casual game" means as the term can be confusing. In "Casual Games Discussion" [14], the following classification is proposed:

- Casual in games cultures: The phenomenon of the casual aspects of games cultures.

- Casual game: Certain properties of games are called casual, e.g., game has generally appealing content, simple controls, easy-to-learn gameplay, fast rewards, or support for short play sessions. These properties can vary depending on the game, and the term should be treated more or less ostensibly.

- Casual gaming. The aspects of the present game cultures are characterized as casual: the attitude towards gaming may be casual, e.g., playing games may be perceived as just one leisure activity among others (e.g., TV, movies, sports) or present clearly instrumental motives other than leisure for the playing activity.

- Casual playing: The way a game is used or played is characterized as casual, e.g., a game is played in small-time bursts or in a low cognitive state. This refers more to the play session than to the general attitude towards games.

- Casual gamer: A person who plays games in a casual manner, not necessarily casual games (casual playing), or who has a casual attitude towards gaming (casual gaming).

- Casual game player: A person who plays games that are called or labeled as casual (not necessarily playing casually). Studies show that the demography covers almost everybody (from teens to older people, from newbies to lapsed gamers) and the largest group seems to be "women over 35."

In this work, we considered World of Warcraft casualization in the sense of taking aspects of "casual games" to provide players a "casual playing" style of play. By any means, we have considered World of Warcraft as a "casual game."

One of the most important works on casual games is the book *A Casual Revolution* by Juul [15]. Its author is a Danish game designer, as well as an educator and video game study theorist. In his book, he explains the growth of casual games, which reach an audience that goes beyond the traditional audience of video games.

This book has had a significant impact, as we can see from the various articles that build on it. An example would be "Congenial by Design: A review of A Casual Revolution" [16]. It is a review of Juul's book focusing on how it addresses the growing popularity of casual games with the advent of the Wii, mobile games, downloadable games, etc. After reviewing several topics covered in the book, the author criticizes some aspects that he thinks should be explored more deeply, although he considers the book indispensable for anyone in the video game industry. Another article based on Juul's book is "Not a Casual Review: Reading Jesper Juul's A Casual Revolution" [17]. Similar to the previous one, it is a review of the book, albeit in greater depth, commenting on part by part and contributing with novel ideas, such as that a hardcore player can play a hardcore game casually.

Related to the casual theme, beyond *A Casual Revolution*, we can find "The Structure of Videogame Preference" [18], where its authors investigate statistical patterns of player preferences around different game aspects. They divide casual players from hardcore players and include a difference between genres. They also deal with other factors such as game theme and popularity. The authors conclude that the player's gender predicts what kind of game they will play, with women being casual games generally. However, in its differentiation between mainstream games and niche games, this difference between genres cannot be seen.

4. Evolution of stats

In this section, we summarize and analyze collected data about World of Warcraft stats system evolution through its different expansions. It's divided into sections corresponding to each one of the studied versions of the game, starting from the launch version known as Vanilla. In each section we summarize the most relevant changes on character stats and analyze them qualitatively, identifying motives behind each change, their in-game effect and their possible contribution to game casualization.

4.1 Vanilla

World of Warcraft's first version is usually called Vanilla version. It was launched in 2004 in America and 2005 in Europe. In Vanilla version, character sheet contains stats, items, and abilities sections. Stats split into primary stats or attributes and secondary stats. There were five attributes: strength, agility, stamina, intellect, and spirit. Increasing an attribute also increased related secondary stats. For example, an increase in stamina also increased life while improving strength also increased attack power. Leveling up the character provides additional primary stats, while equipment can increase both primary and secondary stats, depending on the equipped items.

Primary	Attack	Defense	Spell offensive	Spell healing	Resistances
Strength	Strength	Stamina	Intellect	Intellect	Fire res
Agility	Agility	Defense	Spell damage	Spirit	Ice res
Stamina	Damage	Armor	Spell hit chance	Healing	Arcane res
Intellect	Attack power	Parry	Spell crit. strike	Spell crit. strike	Nature res
Spirit	Attack hit chance	Dodge	Spell haste	Spell haste	Shadow res
	Attack crit. strike	Block value	Spell penetration	Mana regen	
	Attack haste				

Table 1.
Role stats in WoW Vanilla.

As secondary "item stats," we can find the following: hit chance, attack power, attack speed, haste, damage, attack critical strike, defense, armor, dodge, parry, block value, spell hit chance, spell power, healing power, spell critical strike, elemental resistances, spell penetration, and mana regeneration. Haste is divided in three stats, for melee, ranged, and spell attacks. In the case of spell damage and elemental resistances, there is one stat for each type of element, these being arcane, fire, nature, frost, and shadows [19]. In total, we can find 28 different "item stats." There are at least eight additional "non-item stats," which are life, mana, energy, rage, attack speed, ranged attack speed, cast speed, health regeneration, and block chance. In **Table 1** we show how all item stats relate to the different roles a player can take during combat.

In this work, we will also consider defense skill and weapon's skills, stats that are increased not by leveling or equipping the character but only when the character defends against attacks or attacks using a particular type of weapon. In Vanilla version there are many different weapon skills, one for every kind of weapon in the game, such as one-handed swords, two-handed swords, staves, or bows. Weapon skills increase the probability of hitting and critically hitting, as well as the damage done with that type of weapon. Defense skill increases the defense stat, which decreases the probability of being hit or critically hit, and also other defensive secondary stats as dodge, parry, and block chance. Weapon and defense skills were, therefore, opposing stats.

Other character aspects that have an impact on stats are race, class, and specialization. Each race had a different effect on character stats and weapon skills. Classes and specializations determine which stats have more importance for the character. For example, some classes based their damage on the strength stat, others on the agility stat, and others on the intellect stat. We will ignore all aspects related to races, classes, and specializations in this study to focus on the changes that have affected all players in general and the different roles that a character can play in combat, regardless of their specific class or race.

4.2 The Burning Crusade

4.2.1 Changes in this expansion

The first expansion of World of Warcraft, The Burning Crusade, is launched in January 2007. The maximum character level is increased from 60 to 70. In this expansion there are some significant changes regarding character stats.

In this expansion some combat-related secondary stats are changed from absolute percentages to arbitrary values that translate to percentages through

Primary	Attack	Defense	Spell offensive	Spell healing	Resistances
Strength	Strength	Stamina	Intellect	Intellect	Fire res
Agility	Agility	Defense	Spell damage	Spirit	Ice res
Stamina	Damage	Armor	Spell hit chance	Healing	Arcane res
Intellect	Attack power	Parry	Spell crit. strike	Spell crit. strike	Nature res
Spirit	Attack hit chance	Dodge	Spell haste	Spell haste	Shadow res
	Attack crit. Strike	Block value	Spell penetration	Mana regen	
	Attack haste				
	Armor penetration				
	Expertise				

New stats in this expansion are underlined.

Table 2.
Role stats in The Burning Crusade.

mathematic formulas, which take character level as a factor. Affected stats are since then called ratings, like hit rating, critical strike rating, dodge rating, or parry rating. During combat these ratings are converted to percentages by applying the mentioned formulas. These formulas use character level as a lowering factor, so that final percentages do not get too high when character level increases.

During the expansion lifecycle, two new stats are added: expertise and armor penetration. Expertise reduces the probability of enemies dodging or parrying melee attacks when attacking them frontally or just dodging when attacking from behind, as in that situation the enemy cannot parry. Armor penetration allows melee attacks to ignore a percentage of the target's armor stat (**Table 2**).

4.2.2 Analysis of changes

The conversion of many stats from absolute percentages to relative ratings occurs with the implementation of the combat rating system [20]. Combat rating system is necessary as the expansion raised the character maximum level from 60 to 70, and, if they did not make this change, absolute percentages would have escalated excessively between level 60 and 70. This change also made it easier to balance the game just by tweaking the formulas.

Expertise reduces the chances of enemy blocking attacks, or parrying attacks when attacking frontally. It is an important benefit for the defensive roles as they always attack from the front but also important for attack roles. Armor penetration helps damaging enemies with high armor, which can help damage-oriented players when facing final bosses. Both stats are cap value stats, which means that when they are improved past a particular value, they stop providing any benefit to the player. This game mechanic increases the complexity of the game, requiring an in-depth knowledge from players to improve related stats optimally.

4.3 Wrath of the Lich King

4.3.1 Changes in this expansion

At the end of 2008 comes the second expansion of World of Warcraft, Wrath of the Lich King. The maximum character level is increased from 70 to 80. It applies some simplifications to the characters' stats. It was in this expansion that the maximum number of players in the history of World of Warcraft was reached [21].

Primary	Attack	Defense	Spell offensive	Spell healing	Resistances
Strength	Strength	Stamina	Intellect	Intellect	Fire res
Agility	Agility	Defense	Spell power ~~Spell damage~~	Spirit	Ice res
Stamina	Damage	Armor	Hit chance ~~Spell hit chance~~	Spell power ~~Healing~~	Arcane res
Intellect	Attack power	Parry	Critical strike ~~Spell crit. strike~~	Critical strike ~~Spell crit. strike~~	Nature res
Spirit	Hit chance ~~Attack hit chance~~	Dodge	Haste ~~Spell haste~~	Haste ~~Spell haste~~	Shadow res
	Critical strike ~~Attack crit. strike~~	Block value	Spell penetration	Mana regen	
	Haste ~~Attack haste~~				
	Armor penetration				
	Expertise				

New stats in this expansion are underlined, removed stats are strikethrough.

Table 3.
Role stats in Wrath of the Lich King.

One notable change is the elimination of weapon skills and defense skill. Since this change, these stats were always considered at the maximum available for the character level.

Besides, some stats are unified and simplified. The physical hit rating is unified with the spell hit rating, leaving only a hit rating for both physical and spell attacks. The same happens with critical strike rating and haste, which were split in two or three different stats and are now unified in this version. Similarly, but affecting only spellcasting classes, all types of elemental spell power are unified and also merged with healing power (**Table 3**).

4.3.2 Analysis of changes

Removing the skill system for both weapons and defense seems to be a change with the sole intention of avoiding players to waste time improving these skills. Before this change, if the character started using a weapon he had never used, he had to spend some time training with that weapon until he was able to use it optimally, which resulted in the player fighting enemies only with melee attacks, trying to lengthen the combat as much as possible to raise the skill. Removing these skills saves players from having to worry about this cumbersome process, allowing them to start using any new weapon optimally right away. Overall, it seems that these changes were beneficial for most players, especially for new ones, and for those who started leveling new characters.

Unification of the hit rating, critical strike rating, and haste between spells and physical attacks had little effect on players. Rarely a character bases his damage both in physical and spell attacks, so unifying both stats was probably done to simplify the system without affecting the gameplay deeply.

Something similar happened with spell power and healing power, but this specific change could have the intention of facilitating hybrid spellcaster to use both damage and healing spells with equal power, fostering the use of both offensive and healing spells to facilitate leveling up. Before this change, leveling up as a healer was a time-consuming task, since he had few ways to kill enemies quickly. After the change, a healing class could also do significant amounts of damage, making it much easier to level up. In general, this change helped players that used healing-focused characters.

Regarding the removal of elemental damage, it meant the end of character builds focused on those stats, like mages that could specialize in fire or ice damage. With this change, all classes and specializations started using the same stat for damage calculations, facilitating their equipment.

4.4 Cataclysm

4.4.1 Changes in this expansion

The third expansion of World of Warcraft was launched in late 2010, called Cataclysm. The maximum character level is increased from 80 to 85. As of the release of this expansion, the number of World of Warcraft subscribers started to decrease progressively.

This expansion eliminates defensive stats on tank characters. Defense and block value are eliminated. The defense function of reducing damage is carried out by other stats, such as armor, parry, or dodge. Block value stat also disappears, making every character to block 30% of the damage by default.

Mana regeneration secondary stat is also eliminated, leaving the spirit as the only source of mana regeneration. Affected classes obtain a new active ability that allows them to increase mana regeneration. Besides, spirit stops giving life regeneration, being now an exclusive stat for mana regeneration.

Attack power is removed from all items, and spell power is left only on weapon items. Both stats can now be improved through character attributes: intellect provides spell power, and strength and agility provide attack power.

The block chance and armor penetration stats are removed from the equipment, keeping them in talents, mastery (see below), and some abilities. Items that lost these stats were compensated with mastery.

A new secondary stat is added: mastery. This stat is different from the rest, since it is associated with a specific effect that depends exclusively on the character specialization. As an example, in one specialization, mastery increases armor penetration, while in another, it increases the block chance. Whatever the effect, mastery is always a passive ability whose effectivity increases with the mastery stat.

Primary	Attack	Defense	Spell offensive	Spell healing	Resistances
Strength	Strength ~~Attack power~~	Stamina	Intellect	Intellect	Fire res
Agility	Agility ~~Attack power~~	~~Defense~~	Spell power	Spirit	Ice res
Stamina	Damage	Armor	Hit chance	Spell power	Arcane res
Intellect	Hit chance	Parry	Critical strike	Critical strike	Nature res
Spirit	Critical strike	Dodge	Spell penetration	Haste	Shadow res
	Haste	~~Block value~~	Haste	~~Mana regen~~	
	~~Armor penetration~~	Mastery	Mastery	Mastery	
	Expertise				
	Mastery				

New stats in this expansion are underlined, removed stats are strikethrough.

Table 4.
Role stats in Cataclysm.

A significant change is made to items and the stats they provide. Since the beginning, every item had an item level and a rarity, which determined the amount of primary and secondary stats it supplied to players. Since this expansion, stats provided by items no longer depend on their rarity and rely exclusively on their item level. Since this change, two items of the same level will give the same amount of primary stats, stamina, and secondary stats, differing only in the type of secondary stats provided (**Table 4**).

4.4.2 Analysis of changes

Most of the changes in this expansion had the effect of making it easier for players to get proper equipment for their characters and to make comparisons between items.

With the removal of block value, it becomes easier to find better shields as they only differ by their item level and the type of secondary stats it provides. When a player had to choose between two shields, the higher the item level of the shield, the better it will be for the player, except for secondary stats, which the player must consider only when there is a scarce difference between the item levels of both shields. This change, besides the elimination of the defense stat, facilitates the equipment of players with a defensive role, as they have fewer stats to consider.

By making mana regeneration depends exclusively on the spirit stat, spirit starts being the most crucial stat for healers and an ignored one by everyone else, which means that any item that provides spirit will be seen in most cases as an item for healers, since they are the only ones that can get a real benefit from it. Healing classes also have some talents that improve damage capabilities based on spirit, helping them to change between damage and healing specializations, especially for leveling up purposes. In general terms, this change makes it easier for healers to get useful items depending only on the spirit they provide.

The fact that the most important stats for damage specializations, attack power and spell power, are obtained only through the character's primary stat greatly increases the importance of that stat. It also simplifies the comparison of different pieces of equipment, because as already stated, items of higher level always provide more primary stats.

Finally, mastery is the first secondary stat in World of Warcraft that is useful for all characters, independently of their class or specialization. It starts a tendency that looks forward to make stats useful for different in-game roles, instead of having role-specific stats. In future expansions, we will see how this tendency is generalized, making almost all stats useful for every character and class.

4.5 Mists of Pandaria

4.5.1 Changes in this expansion

The fourth expansion of World of Warcraft is launched in late 2012. The maximum character level is increased from 85 to 90. In this expansion some stats are eliminated, and there are relevant changes in PvP stats.

As it previously happened with elemental spell power, elemental resistance stats are also eliminated in this expansion, leaving them only on certain spells and racial traits and overall reducing their impact and importance. Spell penetration, a secondary stat designed to surpass elemental resistances, is also eliminated.

Another change is that intellect stops giving maximum mana. From now on, it will only provide spell power and critical strike rating. The maximum amount of mana of a character depends solely on its level and increases considerably with

Primary	Attack	Defense	Spell offensive	Spell healing	Resistances
Strength	Strength	Stamina	Intellect	Intellect	~~Fire res~~
Agility	Agility	Armor	Spell power	Spirit	~~Ice res~~
Stamina	Damage	Parry	Hit chance	Spell power	~~Arcane res~~
Intellect	Hit chance	Dodge	Critical strike	Critical strike	~~Nature res~~
Spirit	Critical strike	Mastery	Haste	Haste	~~Shadow res~~
	Haste		Mastery	Mastery	
	Expertise		~~Spell penetration~~		
	Mastery				

New stats in this expansion are underlined, removed stats are strikethrough.

Table 5.
Role stats in Mists of Pandaria.

each level up, not becoming a cause of problems for mana-dependent classes anymore (**Table 5**).

4.5.2 Analysis of changes

According to developers [22], elemental resistances are eliminated because they were difficult to understand. Although potentially interesting, they were not using them in World of Warcraft and therefore decided to remove them. Once the resistances have been eliminated, magic penetration has no use and is also removed. With the elimination of the resistances, players no longer need to have a specific set of items with elemental resistances exclusively for some end-game encounters. There were rare cases in which this happened, mostly in Vanilla and Wrath of the Lich King expansions, but this type of battle did not happen in the last expansions. Resistances' removal thus facilitates equipping characters for end-game content, making them know that elemental resistances are something that they will not have to care about anymore. As in fact, elemental resistances were not being used in recent expansions of end-game content, the change has little impact on gameplay.

The simplification of intellect primary stat, removing its relationship with mana, allows game designers to control the exact amount of mana that each specialization will have available, as it no longer will depend on equipped items. In any case, the stat is still one of the most important for players, as it is the main form of improving damage and healing for spell casters, so the change does not have a substantial impact on gameplay.

4.6 Warlords of Draenor

4.6.1 Changes in this expansion

At the end of 2014 comes Warlords of Draenor, the fifth expansion of World of Warcraft, which aims to return somewhat to the roots of the game. The maximum character level is increased from 90 to 100. Many stats are removed, while new ones are added. A compression in stats also occurs for the first time.

Hit and expertise ratings are eliminated from the game and from the formulas used when hitting. That is, when a character attacks, the only thing that is considered to see if the attack fails to hit is the difference in level between the attacker and its target. It must be clarified that when an attack does not fail, it is still necessary to check whether it is dodged, parried, or blocked.

Primary	Attack	Defense	Spell offensive	Spell healing
Strength	Strength/agility	Stamina	Intellect	Intellect
Agility	Damage	Armor	Spell power	Spirit
Stamina	~~Hit chance~~	~~Parry~~	~~Hit chance~~	Spell power
Intellect	Critical strike	~~Dodge~~	Critical strike	Critical strike
Spirit	Haste	Mastery	Haste	Haste
	~~Expertise~~	Versatility	Mastery	Mastery
	Mastery	Bonus armor	Versatility	Versatility
	Versatility			
	Multistrike			

New stats in this expansion are underlined, removed stats are strikethrough.

Table 6.
Role stats in Warlords of Draenor.

Dodge and parry ratings are removed from the items, and, instead, they start to depend on abilities, talents, and primary stats, such as agility, which increases the dodge rating, and the strength, which increases the parry rating. It's a similar change to the one suffered by attack power in Cataclysm expansion but now with defensive stats.

Agility and intellect stop giving critical strike rating. This change is compensated by adding a 5% base critical strike rating to all classes and a passive ability for all agility-based classes that increases critical strike rating by another 5% extra. With this change, all the uses that the intellect attribute had in the original version of World of Warcraft have been eliminated.

New secondary stats are added in this expansion: bonus armor, multistrike, and versatility. A new type of stats, tertiary, is also introduced with avoidance, indestructible, leech, and speed, which have less in-game effect than the secondary stats.

Finally, from this expansion onwards, items stop giving a particular primary stat, and, instead, they provide the most relevant primary stat for the character's specialization. In the same object, a mage sees that it gives intellect, and a warrior sees that it provides strength (**Table 6**).

4.6.2 Analysis of changes

According to patch notes [23], the elimination of the hit rating and the expertise is due to the game mechanics not being fun, since the goal of both stats was to remove a penalty, avoiding attack fail and attack being parried or dodged, respectively, and not to obtain an advantage. Therefore, designers decided to eliminate them from the game. In the case of the hit rating, now all attacks have a 100% chance of hitting. In the case of expertise, the probability of being parried when attacking ahead is fixed at 3%. Eliminating expertise and hit ratings removes the need for damage specializations to maximize those stats to a certain level to be fully effective when attacking. This way, players can center their efforts on the improvement of stats that increase the attack damage, no longer worrying about cap values for hit rate and expertise. Cap value was the maximum amount that a character should have in a stat to perform at the best level. Any additional rating above the cap had no in-game effects, so players needed a depth knowledge to avoid having an excessive rating that could be better used for other secondary stats.

In the case of dodge and parry ratings, stats focused on tanks, designers decide to eliminate them in exchange for the bonus armor, a tank exclusive stat. In the patch notes, they explain that they want to keep these stats in low numbers, to avoid the tanks receiving damage peaks, and to make their life more stable. This will happen since the defense stat reduces all damage taken by a percentage, while dodge and parry ratings were based on attack avoidance. Previously, with high dodge and parry values, tanks could avoid many of the attacks received, but those blows that hit caused a lot of damage. Now, with the removal of dodge and parry ratings in exchange for bonus armor, tanks receive damage over time more homogenously. This change simplifies equipping, as previously a player could be interested in an item depending on whether it improved parry or dodge ratings, and now the only option to consider is the bonus armor. Also, as the life is more stable, the work of the healer, who has more reaction time, is facilitated, and, in general, it will be easier to save someone who is receiving a lot of damage.

The elimination of the critical strike chance from agility and intellect is done to compensate for their difference with strength stat, which did not provide critical strike chance. This difference in primary stats made it challenging to balance primary and secondary stats. This simplification and the changes in equipment, which now adapts the primary stat provided to the specialization of the character using it, make strength and agility almost indistinguishable and facilitate, even more, the task of equipping a character.

Regarding the remaining new stats, versatility, in the same way that mastery, is a useful stat in every class and specialization, as it improves both damage, healing, and damage reduction. It's challenging to discover the reasons why multistrike was added, as it's similar to critical strike, and, in fact, it will be removed in the next expansion. The tertiary stats are merely small and random bonuses for items, which do not have a very considerable impact but that are appreciated when they appear.

4.7 Legion

4.7.1 Changes in this expansion

The sixth expansion of World of Warcraft is launched in 2016, Legion. The maximum character level is increased from 100 to 110. It makes few changes in the stats, except to discard some of those introduced in the previous expansion.

The spirit is removed, thus finishing with the possibility of improving mana regeneration through attributes. Mana regeneration, so crucial for healing classes, is no longer a stat and depends on abilities, talents, and items. Besides, the base mana regeneration for healing classes is increased.

Spell power is removed from the items (from weapons that provided it) and now can only be increased with intellect. This way, it suffers the same change that happened to attack power stat in Cataclysm.

Some other stats introduced in Warlords of Draenor are eliminated: bonus armor and multistrike. Only versatility and tertiary stats remain. All these stats are replaced by versatility, which in turn gets much more important than before (**Table** 7).

4.7.2 Analysis of changes

As developers explain in patch notes, the elimination of both the spirit and the bonus armor is done to reduce the amount of equipment changes between specializations, that is to say, to make the equipment carried by a healer or a tank to be also useful for damage specializations. This change facilitates equipping characters, allowing players to change specialization easily without needing to find specific items to play that role successfully.

Primary	Attack	Defense	Spell offensive	Spell healing
Strength	Strength/agility	Stamina	Intellect	Intellect
Agility	Damage	Armor	~~Spell power~~	~~Spirit~~
Stamina	Critical strike	Mastery	Critical strike	~~Spell power~~
Intellect	Haste	Versatility	Haste	Critical strike
~~Spirit~~	Mastery	~~Bonus armor~~	Mastery	Haste
	Versatility		Versatility	Mastery
	~~Multistrike~~			Versatility

New stats are underlined and removed stats are strikethrough.

Table 7.
Role stats in Legion.

By eliminating the spirit of the objects, the regeneration of mana of many specializations must be compensated. The change requires mana user to manage mana with more care and more actively, as its regeneration now depends on abilities, talents, objects, potions, etc., complicating their labor.

The removal of spell power from item seems natural, as it already happened with attack power. Intellect providing mana and critical chance was the only reason to avoid the unification of intellect and spell power, but since the simplifications of primary stats that happened on Warlords of Draenor, their unification was expected.

Finally, secondary stats are adjusted to make them less relevant. Now the most crucial thing regarding item comparison is their item level, and rarely an item with lower level will have more benefits than a higher level one. This facilitates character equipping enormously.

5. Discussion

In the previous sections, we have identified and qualitatively analyzed changes to the combat stats trough expansions. While it's apparent that stats and their related game mechanics have been simplified, in this section we will expose the quantitative analysis that will allow us to see this relationship clearly and to respond to the research questions.

In **Figure 1**, we can see that in every expansion since The Burning Crusade, the number of "item stats," which are those that can be directly increased by the player, has been reduced. In Legion, the last expansion analyzed in this work, the total amount of stats is 1/3 of the amount found in the first expansion. Some item stats were unified, others eliminated, and some others removed from items and included as effects of other game mechanics that depended on the character level, something we will discuss further later.

In **Figure 2** we can see that, besides reducing the total amount of item stats, the number of stats required to play a role optimally has also been reduced, especially if we compare The Burning Crusade expansion, were the stat system had more complexity, to Legion, the last expansion analyzed. The number of stats that the player had to pay attention to when equipping his character has been reduced by 3 for the attack role, 2 for the defense and spell healing roles, or 1 for the spell offensive role. We can now answer research question 1.1, confirming that the number of stats required to play optimally has been reduced.

Regarding research question 1.2, we have to pay attention to the stats that have been moved from the "item stats" group to the "non-item stats" group. Many of the

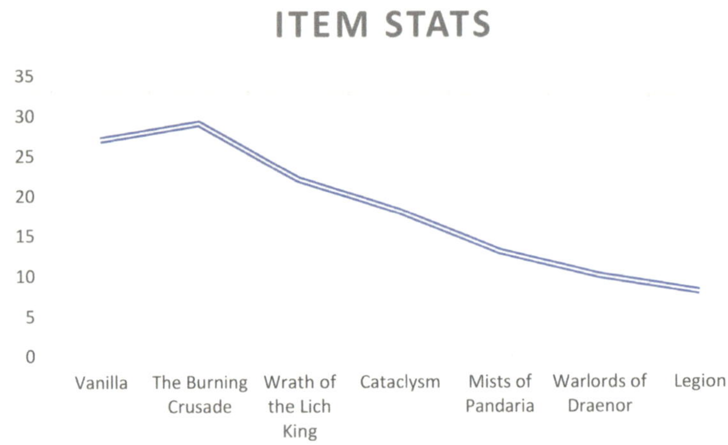

Figure 1.
Amount of item stats through expansions.

	Attack stats	Defense stats	Spell offensive stats	Spell healing stats
Vanilla	7	6	6	6
The Burning Crusade	9	6	6	6
Wrath of the Lich King	9	6	6	5
Cataclysm	8	5	7	5
Mists of Pandaria	8	5	6	5
Warlords of Draenor	6	5	6	6
Legion	6	4	5	4

Figure 2.
Amount of item stats specific for each role through expansions.

stats that were initially obtained through the items were moved to other game mechanics, such as talents and abilities, which depend on the character level. As players can obtain character levels much more easily than good items, this change can be understood as a facilitation for players to increase certain stats. But this conclusion can be argued to be wrong, as talents and abilities have their own complexities. Talents require the player to make adequate decisions for his character, choosing some talents and leaving others out, while abilities require an active behavior from players in combat by activating the corresponding ability when they think it will be more useful. So instead of concluding that these changes have facilitated the increase of stats, it would be more appropriate just to say that the importance of items for stat obtention has been reduced in favor of other game mechanics (**Figure 3**).

Another way in which the obtention of stats has been facilitated is by making all stats useful for all characters. As we can see in **Table 8**, in Legion expansion there are scarce differences between the stats that are required to play different roles optimally. In the case of attack, spell offensive, and spell healing, the required stats are almost equal, knowing that items provide the primary stat that better suits the

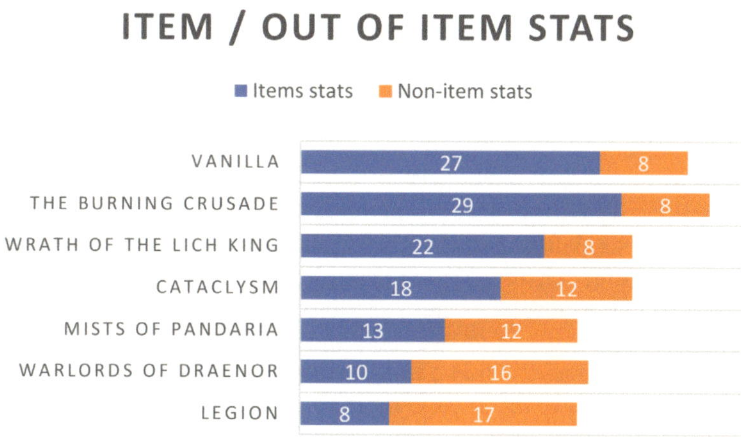

Figure 3.
Comparison between item and non-item stats through expansions.

Primary	Attack	Defense	Spell offensive	Spell healing
Strength	Strength/agility	Stamina	Intellect	Intellect
Agility	Damage	Armor		
Stamina	Critical strike		Critical strike	Critical strike
Intellect	Haste		Haste	Haste
	Mastery	Mastery	Mastery	Mastery
	Versatility	Versatility	Versatility	Versatility

Table 8.
Comparison of role stats in Legion.

character role, so the differences between strength, agility, and intellect are nonexistent. In the case of the defense role, it has even fewer stats to consider than their counterparts. The lack of variety in the role stats facilitates the increase of stats in two ways. First, when a player decides to change his character's role in combat, drastically reducing the need to find appropriate items to play different roles optimally, and second, by reducing the number of attempts required to find an item that suits the character role. With few possibilities, it's more probable that the random secondary stats provided by an item result useful for the character. While in the previous versions of the game a player had to beat a boss multiple times to find a good item that had all the stats required for his role, in the last versions, it's far more easy that he finds a suitable item in the first or second attempt. From this perspective, it is clear that the obtention of stats has been facilitated through the expansions.

Finally, to answer question 1.3, we must go back to the qualitative analysis of expansions made in the previous sections, where we have discussed many mechanical changes to the stats and combat systems. The elimination of the skill system simplified the combat by allowing every character to use any weapon and to defend optimally without previous training. The removal of stats that had a cap value reduced the knowledge and planning required to increase stats optimally for the character role, facilitating the game for new players and for those that were not interested in such in-depth details of the game mechanics.

Changes in defense role stats have also simplified the role of defensive and healing characters in combat, by reducing peak damage on defenders, giving more time for healers to heal them. Changes in mana-related stats, as spirit, mana regeneration, and intellect, also reduced their importance in combat. On the other hand, the addition of mastery stat could be considered as an increase in the complexity of combat, as its effect depends on the character specialization and usually requires to adopt specific behaviors in combat to get more benefit from it.

In general term, we can conclude that the stats and combat game mechanics have been facilitated for new players and casual players by removing some of the most complex or time-consuming stats and their associated game mechanics in combat. But we cannot conclude that the simplification has happened for every player though, as, for example, mastery requires a more active behavior in combat, and the elimination of some defensive- and mana-related stats could have been compensated with changes in other game mechanics, such as talents and abilities. It would be required to study these game mechanics to determine if the combat system has been simplified or not in general terms.

6. Conclusions

Throughout this work, we have analyzed how the World of Warcraft stats system has evolved along successive expansions and updates. We aimed to determine if World of Warcraft has suffered a casualization process by simplifying its stats system, making it easier to understand and use by casual players.

The results show that the number and variety of stats that a player must pay attention to, in order to play optimally, has been significantly reduced. The reduction has happened by unifying and removing stats and by translating stats acquisition from items to other game mechanics. The translation of some stats to talents and abilities facilitates their acquisition, but, at the same time, they come with their own complexities, so we cannot consider this a simplification without a broader analysis. The reduction of the variety of stats that can be found on items does contribute to the casualization of the game, making it much easier for the player to change the specialization of his character without additional efforts required to obtain appropriate items and also reducing the effort required for any player to find suitable items for his character and specialization. Finally, we have also identified some mechanical changes that have contributed to the casualization of the stats and combat systems, making them easier to understand and use for the new and casual players, such as the disappearance of the skill system, the elimination of stats with cap values, or the removal of many defensive- and mana-related stats.

As limitations of this study, we can consider its scope, which does not cover the study of other combat-related game systems such as talents and abilities. Additional studies would be required to understand if the combat system has been casualized in general terms, looking beyond its relationship with the stats system.

The implications of the study are as follows: (1) the number of stats has been reduced in quantity, variety, and complexity along expansions. (2) The increase of character stats has been facilitated by making most of them useful for any character, independently of his role. (3) The stats system has been simplified for new and casual players by removing some complex to understand and time-consuming game mechanics. This study contributes to the field of game design by providing detailed insights on the evolution and casualization of one of the most important videogames in recent years. The results and conclusions of this study could be useful for game designers when designing stats and other related complex systems, discovering different ways in which those systems can be simplified and made more accessible for new and casual players.

As future work, we suggest the study of the evolution of other parts of the combat system of World of Warcraft, such as abilities and talents, or the PVP combat, as well as the study of the evolution of other parts of the game, such as the professions, economy, or guild system. We also consider that this type of study could also be applied to the game series that have suffered an evolution along their different sequels, like Diablo or The Elder Scrolls, to understand in which ways they have changed with the pass of time.

Author details

Adrián Domínguez[1*], Daniel Vallés-Blanco[2], Luis de-Marcos[1], Juan Aguado-Delgado[1] and Sergio Caro-Alvaro[1]

1 Departamento de Ciencias de la Computación, Escuela Politécnica Superior, Universidad de Alcalá, Alcalá de Henares, Madrid, España

2 Centro Universitario en Tecnología y Arte Digital (U-Tad), Universidad Camilo José Cela, Las Rozas, Madrid, España

*Address all correspondence to: adrian.dominguez@uah.es

References

[1] Delmas G, Champagnat R, Augeraud M. From tabletop RPG to interactive storytelling: Definition of a story manager for videogames. Lecture Notes in Computer Science (including subseries Lecture Notes in Artificial Intelligence and Lecture Notes in Bioinformatics). Vol. 5915 LNCS; 2009. pp. 121-126

[2] Apperley TH. Genre and game studies: Toward a critical approach to video game genres. Simulation and Gaming. 2006;**37**(1):6-23

[3] Peckham M. The Inexorable Decline of World of Warcraft. TIME.com. 2013 [Online]. Available from: http://techland.time.com/2013/05/09/the-inexorable-decline-of-world-of-warcraft/ [Accessed: 13 December 2019]

[4] Salen K, Zimmerman E. Rules of Play: Game Design Fundamentals. Cambridge: The MIT Press; 2003

[5] Tan CT, Cheng H. Personality-based adaptation for teamwork in game agents. In: Proceedings of the Third AAAI Conference on Artificial Intelligence and Interactive Digital Entertainment; 2007. pp. 37-42

[6] Glenday C. Guinness World Records Gamer's Edition 2008. London: Jim Pattison Group; 2008

[7] Pietschmann D, Liebold B, Valtin G. The MMORPG designer's journey. New Perspectives on the Social Aspects of Digital Gaming. Routledge; 2018. pp. 82-96

[8] Thurau C, Bauckhage C. Analyzing the evolution of social groups in world of warcraft®. In: Proceedings of the 2010 IEEE Conference on Computational Intelligence and Games, CIG2010; 2010. pp. 170-177

[9] Chen MG. Communication, coordination, and camaraderie in world of warcraft. Games and Culture. 2008; **4**(1):47-73

[10] Bosser AG, Nakatsu R. Hardcore gamers and casual gamers playing online together. Lecture Notes in Computer Science (including subseries Lecture Notes in Artificial Intelligence and Lecture Notes in Bioinformatics). Vol. 4161 LNCS; 2006. pp. 374-377

[11] Paul CA. Game studies – Optimizing play: How theorycraft changes gameplay and design. Game Studies. 2011;**11**(2)

[12] Nutt C. GDC: Learning from world of warcraft's quest design mistakes. Gamasutra. 2009 [Online]. Available from: https://www.gamasutra.com/view/news/113897/GDC_Learning_From_World_of_Warcrafts_Quest_Design_Mistakes.php [Accessed: 13 December 2019]

[13] Josh B. The warning of the world of warcraft effect. Gamasutra. 2018 [Online]. Available from: https://www.gamasutra.com/blogs/JoshBycer/20180718/322337/The_Warning_of_the_World_of_Warcraft_Effect.php [Accessed: 13 December 2019]

[14] Kuittinen J, Kultima A, Niemelä J, Paavilainen J. Casual games discussion. In: Proceedings of the 2007 Conference on Future Play, Future Play '07; 2007. pp. 105-112

[15] Juul J. A Casual Revolution: Reinventing Video Games and Their Players. London: MIT Press; 2010

[16] Woods S. Congenial by design: A review of a casual revolution. Game Studies. 2011;**11**(2)

[17] Björk S. Not a casual review: Reading Jesper Juul's a casual revolution. Game Studies. 2011;**11**(2)

[18] Klevjer R, Hodven JF. The structure of videogame preference. Game Studies. 2017;**17**(2)

[19] Neryssa. Overview of stats on classic WoW. Wowhead. 2019 [Online]. Available from: https://es.classic.wowhead.com/guides/classic-wow-stats-and-attributes-overview [Accessed: 13 December 2019]

[20] Nelson D. Combat rating system explained. Engadget. 2006 [Online]. Available from: https://www.engadget.com/2006/10/16/combat-rating-system-explained/ [Accessed: 13 December 2019]

[21] Prescott S. World of warcraft subscriptions have nearly halved since 2010. PC Gamer. 2014 [Online]. Available from: https://www.pcgamer.com/world-of-warcraft-now-has-6-8-million-subscribers-half-compared-to-2010/ [Accessed: 13 December 2019]

[22] Street G. Coffee with the Devs — Mists of Pandaria Stat Changes. WorldOfWarcraft.com. 2012 [Online]. Available from: https://worldofwarcraft.com/en-gb/news/10036161/coffee-with-the-devs-mists-of-pandaria-stat-changes [Accessed: 13 December 2019]

[23] Ng C. The Iron Tide: 6.0.2 Patch Notes. World Of Warcraft.com. 2014 [Online]. Available from: https://worldofwarcraft.com/en-gb/news/15682579/the-iron-tide-6-0-2-patch-notes [Accessed: 13 December 2019]

Chapter 8

An Evaluation of Game Usability in Shared Mixed and Virtual Environments

Francesco De Pace, Federico Manuri, Andrea Sanna and Iñigo Lerga Valencia

Abstract

Augmented reality (AR) and virtual reality (VR) technologies are increasingly becoming more pervasive and important in the information technology area. Thanks to the technological improvements, desktop interfaces are being replaced by immersive VR devices that offer a more compelling game experience. AR games have started to draw attention of researchers and companies for their ability to exploit both the real and virtual environments. New fascinating challenges are generated by the possibility of designing hybrid games that allow several users to access shared environments exploiting the features of both AR and VR devices. However, the user experience and usability can be affected by several parameters, such as the field of view (FoV) of the employed devices or the realism of the scene. The work presented in this chapter aims to assess the impact of the FoV on the usability of the interfaces in a first-person shooter game. Two players, interacting with AR (first player) and VR (second player) devices, can fight each other in a large game environment. Although we cannot ascertain that different FoVs have affected the game usability, users considered the narrow FoV interfaces to be less usable, even though they could freely move around the real environment.

Keywords: augmented reality, virtual reality, mixed reality, field of view, usability, shared virtual environment

1. Introduction

Figures of the video game market are impressive: it is expected to be worth over 90 billion US dollars by 2020 (BestTheNews, 2016).[1] A significant cut is related to immersive virtual reality (VR) and augmented reality (AR) games. Moreover, technological improvements related to off-the-shelf devices opened new perspectives for researchers and developers to propose users different and intriguing game experiences.

This work presents issues related to the design and the implementation of shared mixed and virtual environments (henceforth referred as hybrid multiplayer games/environments) where players using immersive VR and AR devices can share the

[1] https://www.wepc.com/news/video-game-statistics/

same environment. If a lot of scientific works and commercial applications are known to provide users virtual and augmented game experiences, just a few attempts have been focused on providing hybrid solutions, thus allowing augmented and virtual players to live a game experience together. A first attempt [1] proposed a hybrid environment for playing a tabletop game: the chess. Users experienced both positive game experiences using AR and VR devices, but the limited field of view (FoV) provided by the AR device (the Microsoft HoloLens) partially limited the usability and hence the game experience.

This work aims to investigate the impact of the FoV on the usability in a hybrid shooter game. In particular the following questions will be addressed:

1. Can the FoV limit the usability of first-person shooter games?

2. Can the freedom of movement mitigate the limited FoV for AR players?

In order to tackle these issues, the interfaces for VR and AR players have been implemented as much similar as possible, thus "isolating" the effect of the FoV on the game usability.

Ten users have been preliminary involved in tests; some users tested alternatively the two interfaces and filled a usability questionnaire after each test. Results show a slight preference for the VR interface, and users have indicated the narrow FoV of the AR device as the most important issue, suggesting that the movement capability has not mitigated the influence of the FoV.

This chapter is organized as follows: Section 2 presents the state of the art of VR and AR games; moreover, previous studies related to the impact of the FoV are considered. Section 3 discusses all challenges involved in the design of hybrid shared environments, whereas Section 4 presents the proposed system and describes how the design challenges have been met. Section 5 shows performed tests and obtained results. Finally, Section 6 presents the conclusions and the future works.

2. Related work

In the following sections, the state of the art related to the AR and VR applications in the game/serious game context is presented.

2.1 VR in serious game

Since the 1990s, immersive VR headsets have been employed for gaming. One of the first examples is the Nintendo Virtual Boy, a 32-bit console capable of displaying stereoscopic contents. Thanks to technological improvements, VR headsets have started to be used for contexts different from the gaming domain (such as training, simulation, etc.), allowing users to experience new typologies of applications. Despite these applications are still based on the game mechanic, their main goal is not the entertainment itself but the creation of learning environments, proposing educational experiences. Analyzing the current state of the art, several examples can be found [2–4]. In [2], an immersive VR environment is employed to assess how perception affects actions in the sport domain. Stone et al. [3] illustrated how immersive VR has been employed in the aviation industry, whereas a VR headset is used in [4] for pain management. An interesting comparison between an approach based on immersive VR environment and one based on traditional educational methods for aviation safety is proposed in [5]. Results show that the VR experience has generated a knowledge gain that remains in time (1 week), whereas it is lost rapidly using traditional methods. Further comparisons between VR and non-VR technologies have been carried out in the game domain to analyze in which way an immersive VR environment differs from a non-VR one and to assess the impact of immersive VR technologies on the game experience [6–8]. In [6], a first-person shooter game is considered to evaluate the game experience using VR and non-VR technologies. Despite results indicate that players have preferred the non-VR environment in terms of usability, the VR environment has been perceived more compelling and attractive. Wilson and McGill [7] proposed a comparison to assess the impact of immersive VR in violent video games. Collected outcomes show how users felt higher presence and body ownership with respect to the non-VR solution, perceiving more violence and thus suggesting changing the game rating. Finally, a comparison between VR and non-VR technologies in multiplayer game is proposed in [8]. Results are in-line with the outcomes of the other presented works, showing that users preferred playing multiplayer games in full VR environments with respect to non-VR systems.

2.2 AR in game

One of the first collaborative gaming in an AR environment dates back to 1998, when Szalavári et al. proposed an AR system to play multiplayer tabletop games [9]. Users had to physically be positioned in the same real room, and they could interact with computer-generated contents using tracked probes. Few years later, Thomas et al. [10] extended the well-known desktop game Quake to an AR scenario, allowing users to play the famous game in the real environment. Original Quake's virtual assets (e.g., monsters, weapons, etc.) were displayed in the real surroundings, and they could be visualized by using a wearable device both indoor and outdoor.

AR technologies have been also used to improve the game experience in outdoor scenarios by using wearable [11] and handheld [12] devices. Despite attention to the game design should be paid to avoid undesired problems [13], new devices (such as the Microsoft HoloLens) have been successfully employed to offer AR game experiences in huge size environments [14]. Concerning indoor environments, Nojima et al. [15] proposed an AR system to augment sports with additional computer-generated contents. A modified version of dodgeball is presented in which players can fight each other through a real ball. Players can detect the damage caused by visualizing health bars positioned above the head of the adversarial players. Regarding video games, a plane detection algorithm is used in [16] to display military virtual assets (e.g., soldiers, enemies, etc.) in an indoor environment. Users, by using a handheld device, can defend their environment against the enemy troops' assault.

2.3 Hybrid AR and VR games

One of the oldest attempts of creating hybrid games dates back to the 1920s, when Thomas et al. improved their AR Quake game, adding support to AR/VR collaborative multiplayer [17]. In addition to a custom haptic gun used to shoot to the monsters, a collaborative modality has been added to the system. Two different players were able to interact with the same virtual contents using an AR device and a desktop interface, respectively. Some years later, Cheok et al. developed a modified version of the Pacman game, allowing different users to interact using AR and VR devices [18]. Two players, using two wearable devices, were able to interact visualizing virtual assets superimposed in the real scenario. Furthermore, a third player, interacting in a VR environment, could help Pacman by suggesting the best way to follow. In [19], several AR and VR devices are employed to offer a cross media experience. Each interface provides users different functionalities, highlighting the peculiarity of each device. Clash tank [20] proposes a slightly different approach. Despite users were positioned in an immersive VR scenario, they could still interact with the real environment by visualizing it through a virtual monitor (an external camera is used to acquire the desired images).

Finally, another approach for using both AR and VR interfaces consists in alternating them according to the game flow [21, 22].

2.4 FoV in AR

Some projects have been found regarding the study of the impact of the FoV on AR applications. In [23], an evaluation of the impact of three different FoVs (small, medium, and large) on target-following task is proposed. Results show that despite small FoVs should be avoided for targeting people, no evidence in improving performances in using large FoVs with respect to medium ones has been found. Similarly, Kishishita et al. [24] assessed the impact of FoV of wide AR display by comparing two different types of labeling techniques (in view and in situ) in a search target scenario. Main outcomes illustrate how in situ labeling discovery rate increases, whereas the one of the in view methods decreases as the FoV angle approaches 100°. The performance of the two methods converges at around 130°. Ren et al. [25] developed a system to emulate different FoVs finding out that a $108 \times 82°$ FoV allowed users to fulfill tasks quicker than using a FoV constrained to $45 \times 30°$. The cognitive cost of using different FoVs is evaluated in [26]. Three different devices have been compared to verify whether distinct devices require different cognitive loads in a button-pressing procedural task. Main results demonstrate that spatial AR required significant less effort than the other devices. Authors suggest that the high cognitive load of narrow FoV devices can be reduced by using more virtual cues to drive the attention of the users.

To the best of authors' knowledge, no study has been found related to the evaluation of the FoV on the usability of a hybrid multiplayer game. Since results of [1] showed how FoV had negatively impacted on the usability of the AR interface in a tabletop game, the work presented in this chapter aims to investigate the impact of FoV on the usability of a game in which players can physically move in a large environment.

3. Design challenges

The realization of hybrid multiplayer environments presents several challenges. Depending on the typology of the game experience that the users want to get, different solutions to distinct problems exist. In the following, some of the most relevant challenges are presented and discussed.

3.1 Game level design challenges

Challenges related to the game level design concern at least two different aspects:

- The environment: how to represent the game map
- The alter ego: how to represent the players' characters

In the following sections, these two aspects are introduced and discussed.

3.1.1 Environment

The environment design challenge is related on how to represent and/or make the game map. For the sake of clarity, a hybrid multiplayer environment composed by an AR and VR player (henceforth called ARP and VRP, respectively) is considered (ARP vs. VRP). Depending on whether the ARP's real environment can be known a priori or not, the complexity of managing the environment may vary. In the first case, if the geometry of the environment is known (e.g., by scanning or by using a map), a virtual representation of the environment's shape can be shared with the VRP. Knowing the shape, the two players can effectively interact in the same environment (the one of the ARP) or in two completely different game maps that share only the same shape. In the second case, the ARP should have enough space to play in a game environment unrelated to his/her real environment (e.g., both players can interact in a virtual maze as long as the ARP has enough space to move and to visualize the virtual contents).

The complexity may even increase if two or more ARPs that are not physically in the same real environment are considered. If it is not possible to determine the environment's shape, all the ARPs should have enough space to play in the shared virtual world. On the other hand, knowing the geometry of their environments, the smallest one should be taken as reference shape or the intersection among the different geometries can be determined and used as reference shape for the game map.

In addition to the shape of the environment, real obstacles should be also considered to properly manage the creation of the hybrid environment. Considering the case of ARP vs. VRP, it should be possible to detect the positions, orientations, and typologies of the obstacles of the scene by scanning the real environment or by using pre-defined maps. Once the obstacles are identified, it should be possible to convey at least two different game experiences: in the first one, there can be a 1:1 match between the obstacles of the ARP and the ones of the VRP (e.g., a real chair in the ARP environment is recreated in the VRP scenario by a virtual chair having the same dimension, position, and orientation). In the second one, the dimensions, positions, and orientations of the virtual obstacles are the same as the real ones, but the virtual obstacles differ for the typology/shape (e.g., a real chair in the ARP environment is represented by a virtual rock in the VRP scenario). Indeed, as the number of ARPs rises, the complexity of the obstacle matching system grows, making arduous finding an effective solution (e.g., two ARPs may have different typologies of obstacles in the same positions or distinct obstacles in different positions). In addition to the real obstacles, virtual objects may be added to improve the game experience, making the game more compelling and attractive.

Finally, the interaction with the real objects of the ARP's environment should be also considered. An ARP's environment can be considered as *static* when no interaction is allowed with the real objects. Their positions and orientations cannot be changed, maintaining handily the synchronization with the VRP's environment. On the other hand, an ARP's environment can be considered as *dynamic* when the positions and orientations of the real objects can be modified. In order to keep synchronized the ARP and VRP environments, sensors should be added to monitor the ARP's environment, increasing the complexity of the environment but ensuring a more engaging game modality.

3.1.2 Alter ego

The alter ego design challenge refers on how to visualize and control the players' characters. It is assumed that at least the position and orientation of all the players can be determined and employed to show the virtual alter egos.

Concerning the visualization, in an ARP versus VRP scenario, it is possible to easily visualize two different virtual characters at the positions of the corresponding players by exploiting the different players' tracked data. On the other hand, if the possibility to visualize virtual characters should be provided to two or more ARPs that are in the same physical space, the position of the virtual alter egos with respect to the real players should be carefully planned. The virtual characters can be superimposed on the real person's body, or they can be positioned at a pre-defined distance from the real player. In the first case, despite the position of the virtual character and the real's one is matched, undesired occlusions can arise that may negatively effect on the visualization of the virtual alter ego. In the second case, the virtual characters can be better visualized than in the first scenario, but the ARPs may not clearly understand to which entity (the real person or the displaced virtual alter ego) to pay attention.

The character's control refers on how to give input and animate the virtual character. Both visualization and control can depend on the tracking approach used to monitor the players' movements and actions. Since the most common AR and VR devices currently available on the market usually differ for the tracking capability (commonly, the VR systems are capable of tracking more body parts than the AR devices), the input modalities and the number of recognizable actions may vary from ARPs to VRPs. As the number of tracked actions increases, the possibility of providing precise input and realistic animation grows. Actions may be tracked by using external marker/markerless systems and/or by using physical joysticks to detect the players' input. In order to reduce the complexity of the management of the character's control, it is possible to employ pre-defined animations that can be visualized every time a certain event arises (e.g., if the displacement speed of the player exceeds a pre-defined threshold, a run animation can be played).

Finally, the user interface (UI) of different devices should be carefully planned to avoid undesired effects. When immersive headset (for the VR) or optical see-through devices (for the AR) are employed, the use of 2D elements for the UI should be avoided. It has been shown that visualizing virtual assets on planes placed at different positions with respect to those of the real objects may generate focal problems and it could reduce the user's attention [27, 28]. Hence, the UI should be designed using only 3D computer-generated contents. On the other hand, when using smartphones or desktop interfaces, 2D UI elements can be employed without incurring in undesired problems.

3.2 AR challenges

AR challenges refer to issues that are strictly related to only the ARP. They can be divided in:

- Reference system: how to correctly align the ARPs in the virtual environment
- Game map restriction: how to prevent ARPs from physically leaving the game environment
- Occlusion: how to manage the occlusion between real and virtual objects
- Spawning points: how to effectively spawn the ARPs in the game environment

These challenges are detailed in the following sections.

3.2.1 Reference system

The reference system challenge refers on how to determine the position and orientation of the ARP with respect to a known reference system. At least two different approaches exist:

1. Marker/object tracking

2. ARP's pre-defined starting position

The first approach relies on the use of marker or markerless technologies. An image target can be positioned at a pre-defined distance from the ARP or in a known and specific position of the real environment. Alternatively, object recognition approaches can be employed to determine the ARP's position and orientation with respect to a known object of the real environment. Indeed, the position of the tracked object with respect to the real environment should be known to correctly align the ARP in the game map. On the other hand, in the second approach, the ARP should start at a pre-defined position (it is assumed that the coordinates of this position with respect to the game environment are known) with a preset orientation.

3.2.2 Game map restriction

The game map restriction challenge concerns how to keep ARPs from getting out from the game map. Whereas in the VRP's environment it is relatively simple to avoid this behavior (it can be managed by the game logic itself), it is not physically possible to avoid ARPs to not enter in areas outside the ones defined for the game. One possible approach is placing peculiar virtual assets in critical positions to attempt to limit the ARP's movements. The design of these assets should refer either to the concept of "forbidden" or to existing real objects that are commonly used to prevent people crossing determined areas (such as barriers or barricades).

3.2.3 Occlusion

The occlusion challenge refers to the problems that arise when a virtual object has to cover a real one (or a part of it) in the ARP's environment; a virtual representation of the real object should be created and superimposed on the real object. Then, the occlusions between the two virtual objects can be easily managed by the game logic itself. In addition, it may be desired to make the virtual representations of the real objects invisible (keeping the occlusions). One possible solution may consist in rendering the virtual objects by modifying the material property of the virtual assets, assigning special materials (e.g., despite the black color is rendered as transparent on the HoloLens device, it ensures to occlude any objects positioned behind the black one).

3.2.4 Spawning points

The management of the spawning points should be carefully considered if two or more ARPs that are positioned in different locations needed to be added in the same virtual environment. In fact, it is possible that despite the ARPs are physically in different positions, they could share the same virtual positions, overlapping in the virtual environment. One possible solution consists of letting know players which positions are already occupied by virtual entities before participating in the game session.

4. The proposed system

Since players interact using different devices, the usability of the proposed system is affected by the typology of interface employed to interact in the virtual environment. Hence, in order to isolate the influence of the FoV, it has been attempted to offer the same game experience, overcoming the intrinsic differences of the employed devices. To achieve this goal, despite the differences related to the hardware and the environments, some design choices have been made to make the interactions and the game maps for AR and VR players as similar as possible.

In the following sections, the hardware and software architecture, along with the interfaces and the game level design, are discussed. Moreover, the choices employed to overcome/mitigate some of the challenges discussed in Section 3 are presented and detailed.

4.1 The system architecture

The system architecture is composed by two different entities: an Oculus Rift connected to an Intel Core i7-7700 (16.0 GB RAM, NVIDIA GeForce GTX 1070 Ti) personal computer (PC) and a Microsoft HoloLens[2] device. The first entity corresponds to the VRP workstation, whereas the second one to the ARP workstation. Both workstations are connected on the same local area network (LAN) using UDP socket connections. In addition to the headset, the VRP workstation is equipped with two infrared sensors and two Oculus Touch controllers. The VRP is thus capable of interacting in the virtual environment using the controllers and the headset tracked by the external sensors. The ARP workstation is equipped with a HoloLens clicker[3] device. It consists of a Bluetooth device used by the ARP to interact with the virtual assets.

The hybrid environment has been developed in C# using Unity 2018.3.4 as integrated development environment (IDE). The VRP workstation acts as a server (specifically as a host), whereas the ARP workstation acts as a client. In order to manage the network connection and to access the data from the two employed hardware, the following libraries have been used:

- The MixedRealityToolkit-Unity 2017.4.3[4] to access the HoloLens hardware data

- The SteamVR Plugin[5] to access the Oculus Rift hardware data

- The Unet Unity API[6] (high-level API) to manage the client-server architecture

In **Figure 1** the system architecture is shown.

In the following sections, the AR and VR interfaces and the methodologies adopted to limit the challenges of Section 3 are presented and detailed.

---

2 https://www.microsoft.com/it-it/hololens

3 https://docs.microsoft.com/en-us/windows/mixed-reality/hardware-accessories

4 https://github.com/microsoft/MixedRealityToolkit-Unity/releases

5 https://assetstore.unity.com/packages/templates/systems/steamvr-plugin-32647

6 https://bitbucket.org/Unity-Technologies/networking/src/2018.3/

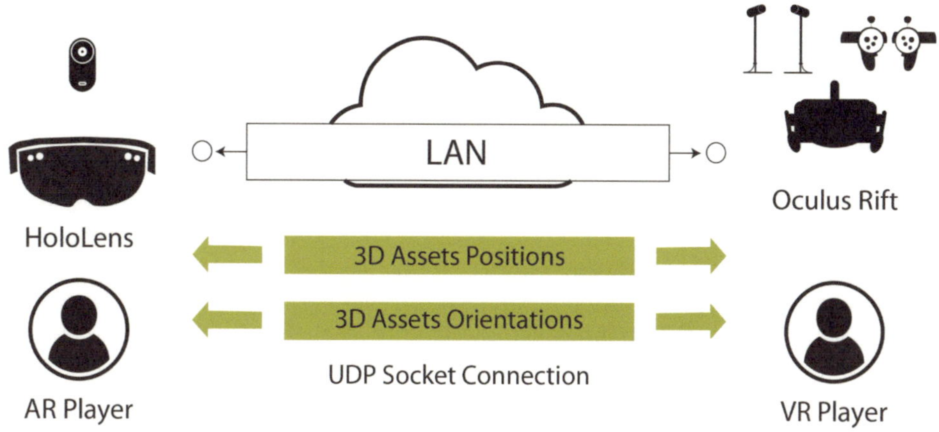

Figure 1.
The system architecture.

4.2 The level design

In order to provide the same interaction to both the ARP and VRP, the interfaces and the game environments have been designed as similar as possible. Several aspects have been considered:

- The proposed alter ego: the player's character and its interaction paradigm
- The proposed UI: the graphic and sound elements that provide information to the players
- The proposed environment: how to represent the game map
- The AR issues

In the following, these aspects are presented and discussed.

4.2.1 The proposed alter ego

The alter ego of both players is represented by a virtual drone. It has been decided to not employ a humanoid (or more articulated) character for two reasons:

Figure 2.
The proposed alter ego.

firstly, to limit the interaction issues (e.g., how the user would control an anthropomorphic character) and secondly due to the narrow FoV of the employed AR device. As stated in [29], a humanoid character can be arduous to be detected using the HoloLens device, and users may be forced to frequently change their point of view to visualize the entire body. Hence, a simpler, smaller, and more visible alter ego has been preferred.

The drone character is capable of flying in all directions, firing from two laser side cannons (**Figure 2**).

To make sure that both players are able to execute these types of actions in a similar way, the character's inputs have been mapped to the alter ego considering the interaction mode of each interface. Specifically, concerning the ARP, the position in the world reference system and the local rotation of the HoloLens have been directly mapped to the drone's global position and local rotation. It is worth to notice that the maximum height reachable from the drone is thus equal to the height of the ARP. The laser fire action has been accomplished exploiting the direction of sight as a gunsight and the button of the HoloLens clicker as a fire button. The capability of gesture recognition of the HoloLens has not been employed as hands can occlude the sight of view and gestures can strain arm muscles. Movements and shooting actions of the VRP have been designed and developed in a similar way. The left Oculus Touch controller and the rotation of the headset have been employed to move the alter ego. More specifically, the rotation of the headset provides the direction of translation, whereas the movement of left joystick along the vertical axis provides the positive or negative magnitude of the translation along the view sight direction. To give the VRP the possibility of moving sideways, the movement of the left joystick along the horizontal axis has been used to provide both the magnitude and the direction of translation. Hence, the VRP is able to move side to side independently of the rotation of the headset. Since the movement's height of the drone controlled by the ARP is constrained by the height of the real AR player, the height of the movement of the VRP's drone has been set to a pre-defined height in order to not allow the VRP to reach areas of the game map not accessible by the ARP (e.g., the ceiling). Finally, the shooting action has been mapped to the trigger

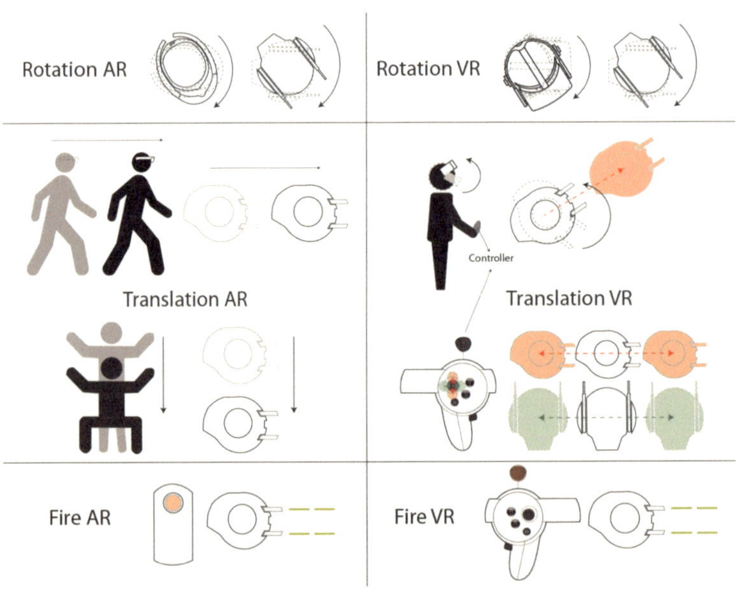

Figure 3.
The AR input mapping (left column) and the VR input mapping (right column).

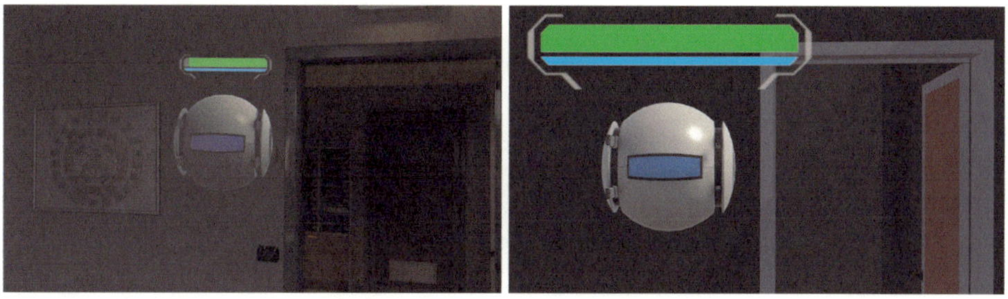

Figure 4.
The AR and VR interfaces.

button of the right Oculus controller, whereas the shooting direction is set by the orientation of the headset. In **Figure 3** the input mapping of both players is shown.

4.2.2 The proposed UI

In order to not occlude the FoV of both devices and to ensure that both players can pay attention to the environment and the game itself, the UI has been kept as minimal as possible. It is essentially composed by three elements that represent the life of the players, the action of being shot, and the action of firing. The players' life is represented by a health bar, positioned at a pre-defined distance from the tip of the drone (see **Figure 2**). To make players aware of being shot, a red panel is rendered for a few moments in front of the camera when the player is hit by a laser shot. The material of the panel is composed by a RGBA color with the alpha channel that has been set to 0.1 (transparent). As the players are being hit, the alpha channel is increased to let the panel being more visible, providing players the sensation of losing life. Finally, a sound of fire is played when the shooting action is executed to improve the realism and the sensation of immersion of the game. In **Figure 4** the two different interfaces can be depicted.

4.2.3 The proposed environment

To attempt to provide the same game experience to both players, it has been decided to create a virtual representation of the ARP's environment by modeling it using Rhino 5[7] and Blender 2.79.[8] The environment consists of two rooms connected by a hallway of Politecnico di Torino. Starting from a detailed map, which included the positions/orientations and typologies of the obstacles (chairs, tables, etc.), a designer has modeled the corresponding virtual environment, matching 1:1 the obstacle-spositions/orientations and typologies of the ARP to the VRP's ones (**Figure 5**).

Considering the adopted client-server architecture, the proposed virtual environment has been employed on the server (the VRP system, acting as a host); thus both virtual representations of the two players can act in the same virtual scenario. The main difference is the visualization of the virtual scenario: it is displayed for the VRP but for the ARP. Hence, the ARP can see the real environments augmented by obstacles with which can "collide." In addition to the aforementioned virtual environment, it has been necessary to employ a scanned version of the same scenario to stabilize the HoloLens tracking; as suggested in [14], a scanned version of the entire real scenario has been made using the HoloLens SLAM capability. Then, the generated model has been used only in the ARP's client application to improve the

[7] https://www.rhino3d.com/it/

[8] https://www.blender.org/

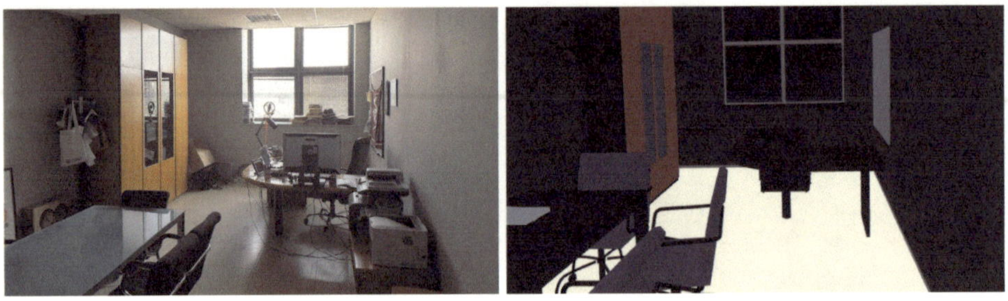

Figure 5.
The real office and its virtual representation. Notice the 1:1 match among the real and virtual objects.

HoloLens' spatial mapping feature, stabilizing the tracking. In **Figure 6**, the modeled and scanned environments and the original map of the Politecnico's rooms are shown.

4.2.4 The proposed solution of the AR issues

Several AR issues have been tried to solve or limit. Concerning the alignment of the reference system, it has been preferred an approach based on the definition of a preset starting position of the ARP with respect to one based on a marker or object tracking. Hence, in order to compute the position and orientation of the HoloLens with respect to the real room, the device is placed on the floor in a preset configuration during the system's booting (**Figure** 7 top-left). When the calibration

Figure 6.
Top-left image: the map used to model the virtual environment. The red zone indicates the game area. Top-right image: the scanned map obtained using the SLAM feature of the HoloLens. Bottom-left image: the virtual environment. Bottom-right image: notice the matching of the virtual environment with the scanned map.

Figure 7.
Top-left image: the pre-defined starting position of the HoloLens. Top-right image: an example of virtual barrier employed to limit the ARP's movements. Bottom-left image: in the background it is possible to visualize the contrast between the real environment and the black material used to make invisible the scanned environment. Bottom-right image: an example of occlusion between a real (the door) and a virtual object (the barrier).

procedure is completed, the ARP can wear the device, and his/her position and orientation can be correctly determined by the system.

In order to prevent the ARP from entering in areas not included in the game environment, some virtual assets, which remind the concepts of "forbidden," "work in progress," or "prohibition," have been added to the game map (see **Figure 7** top-left). They have been positioned in front of closed doors or corners in which players should not pass.

Finally, to properly manage the occlusions among real and virtual objects, the material of the scanned version of the room employed to stabilize the HoloLens tracking has been modified (see Section 4.2.3). It has been changed to pure black to make it transparent, allowing to visualize the real objects and occluding the virtual ones at a time (see **Figure 7** bottom-left and bottom-right).

4.3 The game modality

The game modality consists of a first-person shooter game, in which two players (the ARP and the VRP) compete one against the other, impersonating two drones.

Figure 8.
A virtual trap positioned on the real floor.

The objective is to eliminate the opponent drone, seeking to stay alive. In order to make the game more engaging, some virtual traps have been added to the virtual environment (they are both visible for both players). The traps are placed in some areas of the floor and wall, and they are activated when a player enters in their range (**Figure 8**). A demonstrative video can be found at the following link.[9]

5. Tests and results

This section presents results obtained by a preliminary study on the usability of the presented hybrid multiplayer game environment. These preliminary tests involved 10 people in 5 different sessions; 2 users tested the system for each session. A test session is split into two different parts. During the first part, the first user plays with the VR device, and the second user plays with the AR device; then after about 10 minutes, users are asked for filling a usability questionnaire [30] (the SUS is a reliable and well-consolidated usability questionnaire). During the second part, users exchange the devices and again play for 10 minutes and then fill the usability questionnaire again. Two questions were added to the usability questionnaire that asks users for explaining the best and the worst element of the AR/VR game for their opinion. Users were PhD or MSc students of the computer science courses, and they all, at least occasionally, use AR and VR technologies. For this reason, the training phase at the beginning of each part was very short and was basically aimed to show users the mechanisms of point and shoot and, only for the VR player, the commands to move the avatar. Users involved in test were nine males and one female with age ranging from 21 to 36 years. All users were volunteers, and they signed the Declaration of Helsinki,[10] thus providing informed consent before tests.

Tables 1 and **2** list results for the augmented and virtual applications, respectively. The mean value μ_{AR} and the variance σ^2_{AR} for the AR application are 27.3 (68.5 normalized in hundredth) and 67.3, respectively, whereas μ_{VR} and variance σ^2_{VR} for the VR application are 30.5 (76.25 normalized in hundredth) and 23.1,

User	Q1	Q2	Q3	Q4	Q5	Q6	Q7	Q8	Q9	Q10
1	3	4	3	4	3	4	4	4	4	4
	1	3	2	4	2	2	3	4	2	4
	2	3	3	1	3	4	2	3	1	1
	1	4	3	3	3	4	3	2	3	4
	1	4	3	4	2	2	3	3	4	4
	2	4	3	4	3	4	3	4	3	4
	2	2	1	2	2	3	3	2	3	4
	2	2	4	1	3	3	4	3	4	4
	0	1	0	1	3	2	0	0	0	1
	1	4	4	3	1	3	4	4	2	4

Table 1.
Results obtained by testing the augmented application.

[9] https://drive.google.com/open?id=14vjNgLnyMWpDameigPPo9OE2eXtwKciN

[10] https://www.wma.net/policies-post/wma-declaration-of-helsinki-ethical-principles-for-medical-research-involving-human-subjects/

User	Q1	Q2	Q3	Q4	Q5	Q6	Q7	Q8	Q9	Q10
1	1	3	3	4	2	2	3	3	3	4
	3	4	3	4	3	2	3	3	3	4
	3	3	3	2	3	4	2	4	3	3
	3	4	3	3	3	4	3	4	3	4
	3	4	3	3	2	2	1	2	2	4
	2	3	3	3	3	3	2	3	2	3
	2	2	3	2	2	1	2	2	3	4
	4	4	4	4	4	4	4	4	4	4
	3	4	3	4	3	4	3	4	2	3
	1	4	4	3	3	2	3	4	4	4

Table 2.
Results obtained by testing the virtual application.

respectively. Under the null hypothesis H_0 that $\mu_{AR} = \mu_{VR}$ and the alternative hypothesis that two means are different, an unpaired student t-test has been performed by obtaining a probability $p = 0.2937$ higher than 5%; therefore the null hypothesis cannot be rejected, and the difference between the two mean values of usability is not statistically significant. It cannot be claimed that an application is more usable than the other one, even if a slight preference for the VR solution can be noticed.

Although the statistical analysis does not provide an evidence of user preference and much more users should be involved in the tests, the comments about the best and the worst elements of both applications provided a very interesting food for thought. Most users indicated the FoV as the main limit of the AR interface (as in [1]): it is very difficult to identify the enemy position in particular when the two opponents are closed. On the other hand, the possibility to move in a real environment is the most appreciated aspect. When using the VR applications, users appreciated the level of realism with which the environment has been modeled, and they found a limit in the mechanism of point (with gaze) implemented for the VR interface. Just one user slightly experienced motion sickness using the VR application.

Finally, it is worth to be noticed that only two AR users exceeded the game area, suggesting that the design of the virtual barriers has proved to be effective to limit the ARPs' movements.

6. Conclusions

This chapter presents a study on the impact of the FoV on the usability in a hybrid AR/VR multiplayer game. Starting from the analysis of the challenges and issues that may arise during the designing of hybrid scenarios, a large environment in which two players can fight each other using AR and VR interfaces has been proposed. In order to isolate the FoV parameter, the game environments and the user interfaces have been designed and developed as similar as possible, overcoming their intrinsic differences. The usability of both interfaces has been evaluated in a first-person shooter game. Although it has not been possible to statistically demonstrate that the FoV has impacted on the usability of the interfaces, the major part of the users has clearly stated that the FoV has negatively impacted on the AR game experience. Nonetheless, they have appreciated the possibility of freely moving in the real environment.

Future works will involve more players, considering more than two players for session and different devices.

Author details

Francesco De Pace*†, Federico Manuri†, Andrea Sanna† and Iñigo Lerga Valencia
Dipartimento di Automatica e Informatica, Politecnico di Torino, Torino, Italy

*Address all correspondence to: francesco.depace@polito.it

† These authors contributed equally.

References

[1] De Pace F, Manuri F, Sanna A, Zappia D. Virtual and augmented reality interfaces in shared game environments: A novel approach. In: Intelligent Technologies for Interactive Entertainment. Cham: Springer; 2018. pp. 137-147

[2] Bideau B, Kulpa R, Vignais N, Brault S, Multon F, Craig C. Using virtual reality to analyze sports performance. IEEE Computer Graphics and Applications. 2009;**30**(2):14-21

[3] Stone RJ, Panfilov PB, Shukshunov VE. Evolution of aerospace simulation: From immersive Virtual Reality to serious games. In: Proceedings of 5th International Conference on Recent Advances in Space Technologies-RAST2011; Piscataway, New Jersey, USA: IEEE; 2011. pp. 655-662

[4] Tong X, Gromala D, Amin A, Choo A. The design of an immersive mobile virtual reality serious game in cardboard head-mounted display for pain management. In: Pervasive Computing Paradigms for Mental Health. Cham: Springer; 2015. pp. 284-293

[5] Chittaro L, Buttussi F. Assessing knowledge retention of an immersive serious game vs. a traditional education method in aviation safety. IEEE Transactions on Visualization and Computer Graphics. 2015;**21**(4): 529-538

[6] Pallavicini F, Ferrari A, Zini A, Garcea G, Zanacchi A, Barone G, et al. What distinguishes a traditional gaming experience from one in virtual reality? An exploratory study. In: Applied Human Factors and Ergonomics. Cham: Springer; 2017. pp. 225-231

[7] Wilson G, McGill M. Violent video games in virtual reality: Re-evaluating the impact and rating of interactive experiences. In: Proceedings of the 2018 Annual Symposium on Computer-Human Interaction in Play; New York, NY, USA: ACM; 2018. pp. 535-548

[8] Christensen JV, Mathiesen M, Poulsen JH, Ustrup EE, Kraus M. Player experience in a VR and non-VR multiplayer game. In: Proceedings of the Virtual Reality International Conference-Laval Virtual; New York, NY, USA: ACM; 2018. p. 10

[9] Szalavári Z, Eckstein E, Gervautz M. Collaborative gaming in augmented reality. In: VRST. Vol. 98; New York, NY, USA: ACM; 1998. pp. 195-204

[10] Thomas B, Close B, Donoghue J, Squires J, De Bondi P, Morris M, et al. ARQuake: An outdoor/indoor augmented reality first person application. In: Digest of Papers. Fourth International Symposium on Wearable Computers; Piscataway, New Jersey, USA: IEEE; 2000. pp. 139-146

[11] Avery B, Piekarski W, Warren J, Thomas BH. Evaluation of user satisfaction and learnability for outdoor augmented reality gaming. In: Proceedings of the 7th Australasian User Interface Conference. Vol. 50; Sydney, Australia: Australian Computer Society, Inc.; 2006. pp. 17-24

[12] Cordeiro D, Correia N, Jesus R. ARZombie: A mobile augmented reality game with multimodal interaction. In: 2015 7th International Conference on Intelligent Technologies for Interactive Entertainment (INTETAIN); Piscataway, New Jersey,USA: IEEE; 2015. pp. 22-31

[13] Bonfert M, Lehne I, Morawe R, Cahnbley M, Zachmann G, Schöning J. Augmented invaders: A mixed reality multiplayer outdoor game. In:

Proceedings of the 23rd ACM Symposium on Virtual Reality Software and Technology; New York, NY, USA: ACM; 2017. p. 48

[14] Rompapas D, Sandor C, Plopski A, Saakes D, Yun DH, Taketomi T, et al. HoloRoyale: A large scale high fidelity augmented reality game. In: The 31st Annual ACM Symposium on User Interface Software and Technology Adjunct Proceedings; New York, NY, USA: ACM; 2018. pp. 163-165

[15] Nojima T, Rebane K, Shijo R, Schewe T, Azuma S, Inoue Y, et al. Designing augmented sports: Merging physical sports and virtual world game concept. In: Human Interface and the Management of Information. Cham: Springer; 2018. pp. 403-414

[16] Sung H, Wang CM. X-portal: Mixed reality for body engagement in new first person game experience. In: 2018 IEEE International Conference on Applied System Invention (ICASI); Piscataway, New Jersey,USA: IEEE; 2018. pp. 1073-1074

[17] Thomas B, Close B, Donoghue J, Squires J, De Bondi P, Piekarski W. First person indoor/outdoor augmented reality application: ARQuake. Personal and Ubiquitous Computing. 2002;**6**(1): 75-86

[18] Cheok AD, Goh KH, Liu W, Farbiz F, Fong SW, Teo SL, et al. Human Pacman: A mobile, wide-area entertainment system based on physical, social, and ubiquitous computing. Personal and Ubiquitous Computing. 2004;**8**(2):71-81

[19] Lindt I, Ohlenburg J, Pankoke-Babatz U, Prinz W, Ghellal S. Combining multiple gaming interfaces in epidemic menace. In: CHI'06 Extended Abstracts on Human Factors in Computing Systems; New York, NY, USA: ACM; 2006. pp. 213-218

[20] Ranade S, Zhang M, Al-Sada M, Urbani J, Nakajima T. Clash tanks: An investigation of virtual and augmented reality gaming experience. In: 2017 Tenth International Conference on Mobile Computing and Ubiquitous Network (ICMU); Piscataway, New Jersey,USA: IEEE; 2017. pp. 1-6

[21] Vera L, Gimeno J, Casas S, García-Pereira I, Portalés C. A hybrid virtual-augmented serious game to improve driving safety awareness. In: Advances in Computer Entertainment. Cham: Springer; 2017. pp. 293-310

[22] Ferdinand P, Müller S, Ritschel T, Wechselberger U. The Eduventure—A new approach of digital game based learning combining virtual and mobile augmented reality games episodes. In: Pre-Conference Workshop Game based Learning of DeLFI 2005 and GMW 2005 Conference; Rostock. Vol. 13. 2005

[23] Ventura J, Jang M, Crain T, Höllerer T, Bowman D. Evaluating the effects of tracker reliability and field of view on a target following task in augmented reality. In: Proceedings of the 16th ACM Symposium on Virtual Reality Software and Technology. New York, USA: ACM; 2009. pp. 151-154

[24] Kishishita N, Kiyokawa K, Orlosky J, Mashita T, Takemura H, Kruijff E. Analysing the effects of a wide field of view augmented reality display on search performance in divided attention tasks. In: 2014 IEEE International Symposium on Mixed and Augmented Reality (ISMAR); Piscataway, New Jersey,USA: IEEE; 2014. pp. 177-186

[25] Ren D, Goldschwendt T, Chang Y, Höllerer T. Evaluating wide-field-of-view augmented reality with mixed reality simulation. In: 2016 IEEE Virtual Reality (VR); Piscataway, New Jersey, USA: IEEE; 2016. pp. 93-102

[26] Baumeister J, Ssin SY, ElSayed NA, Dorrian J, Webb DP, Walsh JA, et al. Cognitive cost of using augmented reality displays. IEEE Transactions on Visualization and Computer Graphics. 2017;**23**(11):2378-2388

[27] Lamberti F, Manuri F, Paravati G, Piumatti G, Sanna A. Using semantics to automatically generate speech interfaces for wearable virtual and augmented reality applications. IEEE Transactions on Human-Machine Systems. 2016; **47**(1):152-164

[28] Keil J, Schmitt F, Engelke T, Graf H, Olbrich M. Augmented reality views: Discussing the utility of visual elements by mediation means in industrial AR from a design perspective. In: Virtual, Augmented and Mixed Reality. Cham: Springer; 2018. pp. 298-312

[29] De Pace F, Manuri F, Sanna A, Zappia D. A comparison between two different approaches for a collaborative mixed-virtual environment in industrial maintenance. Frontiers in Robotics and AI. 2019;**6**:18

[30] Brooke J et al. SUS-A quick and dirty usability scale. Usability Evaluation in Industry. 1996;**189**(194): 4-7